Santa And The Business Of Being Santa

Santa Bertram Gordon Bailey, R.B.S.

Santa And The Business Of Being Santa

Published by:

NORTH POLE PUBLISHING HOUSE
4726 Stage Road, Suite #1
Memphis, Tennessee 38128

Copyright © 2014 by the author, Santa Bertram Gordon Bailey, R.B.S.

Cover Art © 2014 by North Pole Publishing Company

Printed in the United States of America

All rights reserved. No part of this publication may be reproduced, stored in retrieval system, or transmitted in any form or by any means-for example, electronic, photocopy, and recording— without the written permission of the Author. The only exception is brief quotations in printed reviews. Such quotations must be used with proper reference to their context and give appropriate credit to their authorship. While the Author has every effort to provide accurate telephone numbers, Internet addresses and other information at the time of publication, neither the publisher nor the Author assumes any responsibility for errors, or for changes that occur after publication. Further, publisher does not have any control over and does not assume any responsibility for Author or third-party websites or their content.

ISBN: 978-0-692-23241-5

Dedication

This book is dedicated to all those who have been called and then accept the challenge to don the red suit and portray Santa Claus as he should be. It is intended to be a guide to those who would willingly:

- follow the precepts of the Santa Claus Oath and bring joy to children of all ages by hearing their dreams,
- attend to the principles of Saint Nicholas, the gift giver, and his generosity.
- support in mind and deed the "real reason for the season", and
- befriend all others within this sacred Brotherhood of Clauses.

In doing all this, and more, this book hopes to help you become a professional Santa Claus, respected by all whom come within your presence, and allow you to spread love, happiness and fulfill the imaginations of the children by becoming the legendary Santa Claus himself.

Contents

Section #1 – Be Original 1

Section #2 – Three Methods Of Learning 3

Section #3 – The Evolution Of The Santa Image 7

Section #4 – The Future of Being Santa 11

Section #5 – The Secret Of Life 17

Section #6 – A Topic That No One Wants To Approach 21

Section #7 – What Separates A "Hobby" Santa From
                A Professional Santa 27

Section #8 – Being A Performer And A Santa 29

Section #9 – Negotiations And The Business Of Being Santa 35

Section #10 – Pricing Your Services 41

Section #11 – Outsource HR/Placement Agencies And How They Work 47

Section #12 – How Your Behavior Can Affect
                 Your Continued Employment 53

Section #13 – Business And The Santa Experience 59

Section #14 – Experience Matters 67

Section #15 – What Can A Santa Do The Rest Of The Year 71

Section #16 – Insurance Sources 77

Section #17 – Ethics-What Are They And How They
                 Apply To The Santa World 81

Section #18 – Taxes And You The Santa 89

Section #19 – The Checklist 97

Section #20 – Magic And Santa 103

Section #21 – Profitable Activities For Mrs. Claus And Elves ... 109

Section #22 – Make-Up And Santa Image Enhancement 115

Section #23 – What Can A Santa Say To Children 119

Section #24 – Storytelling By Santa-An Introduction 125

Section #25 – The Origin Of Santa Claus 129

Section #26 – Traditions 133

Section #27 – My First Name 137

Section #28 – The Elves, Mrs. Claus And Treats 141

Section #29 – Mrs. Claus 148

Section #30 – The Export Of Santa To Other Countries 145

Section #31 – Live Appearances Of Santa In America-A Timeline 149

Section #32 – The Changing Image And Traditions Surrounding Santa Claus As Opposed To St. Nicholas And "Old World Traditions 153

Section #33 – How Traditions Of The Old World And New World Applied To Santa Claus 157

Section #34 – Personal Encounters 163

Acknowledgements

Santa Gordon wishes to thanks the following businesses for their continuing support in the creation and development of Santa and the Business of Being Santa schools concept. I am pleased to acknowledge and recommend these companies. Your patronage of these websites will, in some small way, also thank them for assisting me.

ToysForSanta.com - Proudly owned and operated by *The Fabled Santa*, Santa Stephen Arnold. This online store carries clever products, many designed by *Fabled Santa* specifically with the Santa Claus community in mind. Please check out their Santa's pilot wings, wonderful reindeer buttons and other coat and clothing buttons, belt buckles and fashion pins – all manufactured to exacting specifications and using top quality materials and finishes.

NationwideSantas.com - Sometime Mrs. Claus, sometime Elf and always Master Juggler (of schedules), owner/operator Gina Bacon provides employment opportunities to members of the Santa community throughout the United States and Canada. Nationwide Santas is a full service Santa Claus company, providing year-round entertainment to their clients. Gina's contracts always have benefits and protections that accrue to the performing artists and the rates she negotiates are often some of the best in the business. Join her organization and receive preferential rates on insurance, background checks and more. Membership is open to all who support the Santa community without discrimination – Real Beard, Designer Beard, Mrs. Claus, Elf and others.

NorthPolePublishingHouse.com - Charles Barnett, *The Servant Santa*, owns and operates this full-service publishing house, and offers assistance with graphics, editing and publishing, both in e-book and printed-cover formats as well as audio books. Thanks Santa Charles for tying everyone's work together in this book.

Thank you Santa Stephen, Santa Charles, and Gina. For each of your individual talents that helped make my dreams and goals come true.

Preface

The information in this book is dated the moment it was written. New information is constantly coming into play and pricing changes come along as time passes from the time this was written. So too, the information on Groups and Organizations changes constantly.

I plan to officially update this book every spring and adding topics to it as well. There may be minor revisions throughout the year. Too, I keep a blog on the Facebook group "Santa and the Business of being Santa" where you will find a wealth of information in the files that may not included in this volume.

The pages of this book are printed with a wide margin at the bottom of each page. This has been done to provide you with an area to write notes or questions and make this book even more of a workbook than simply an informational manuscript.

I have been observing the Santa Industry for over 18 years as of this writing and a performing Santa since 1980. I started out as a 'Traditional" bearded Santa and in 1991, I grew out my beard to become a "Real" bearded Santa.

About The Author

Santa Gordon Bailey, owner and head instructor for the Santa and the Business of Being Santa School, has been a professional Santa Claus for thirty-four years. Additionally, he is a trained clown, experienced performing magician and a talented balloon artist.

Just some of his experiences include:

- Member of AORBS through 2008, FORBS to 2012, and IBRBS from 2012 to present
- Nationwide Santa Member # R1
- Lecturer for IUSC from the first class held at the University of Southern California
- Double Lecturer at the Branson Santa Convention in 2006
- Lecturer for FORBS Reunion Luncheons through 2012
- Lecturer at FORBS regional Reunion Luncheons 2013
- Contributing writer to the Magic Castle Library
- Lectures on topics coving Performance Parlor, Magic Performance, Close-Up Magic Performance, Walk Around Magic
- Animal Balloons, Face Painting, Clowning Impromptu and Improvisation Performance, Comedy, Make up Application for Clowns
- Make up Application for Trauma Simulation
- Life style difference between 15th Century Peasantry and 21st Century America
- Multiple topics relating to performing as Santa
- Performed as a Professional Clown, Magician, Wizard, Pirate, Ogre, 15th Cen. Peasant, Face Painter, Balloon Busker, Story Teller and Santa since 1981

As Santa, his experience has included home visits with one family being a repeat visit for 24 years every Christmas Eve. During 2007 season, the last year of home visits, he participated in 130 visits. Additionally, Santa Gordon has done corporate parties, team formation, setting up and hiring groups of entertainers to do large corporate events, including professional photographers, Mrs. Clauses, Craft and Face Painting Elves, Storytelling Elves, Magic, performing Dickens players, and corporate Christmas parties. Since 2008, he has provided Santa portrayals working Malls and other high volume venue locations.

Kids gather round for story time with Santa Gordon

SECTION #1: Be Original

This Topic was originally written for Magicians but it has applications to all performers, even Santa.

The Tarbell Course of Magic is one of the most complete written instructional sources available to the lay public on the subject of Performance Magic with 8 volumes in all. It is like an encyclopedia of Magic but much of the lessons contained are usable in regular everyday life.

In Vol.2, Harlan Tarbell wrote about *Originality*: "The tendency is for the average person to imitate. He sees a performer feature something and then wants to go out and duplicate it. He gets out his notebook and tries to copy the patter word for word. He imitates the performer's gestures, when perhaps these words, these gestures and that mystery are not adapted to his particular personality and therefore looks ludicrous and out of place."

This applies to just about every facet of life. If you are a Santa, you cannot help but be an imitation in the beginning of your portrayal but as you develop your skills and expand your knowledge of the traditions and history of St. Nicholas, you become more of an individual with personality and flair.

Do not go out and buy every nifty item you see other Santas using and or wearing. It may not fit in your presentation. Look at the basics first and give yourself a solid grounding before you buy the $1500 suit, the $400 pair of boots, the $200 laser light up walking stick and the $300 giant "Santa" belt buckle along with all the other accessories and adornments you see others wearing. No matter how much you spend on your appearance, if you do not have the basic skills and knowledge that suit and stuff will only carry you through the first 5 minutes of the show.

After that, you have to do the work of performance.

ARTIST STATEMENT

I do the work because I want to.
I do the work because I like to.
I do the work as a personal exploration of myself.
I do the work to engage other people in thought,
perception and emotion.
I do the work because I have something to say.
I do the work because I have seen something beautiful.
I do the work because I have seen something ugly.
I do the work to be the kind of person I want to be.
I do the work because I know how.
I do the work to make money.
I do the work because I am an Artist.

W. Dan Cantrell

SECTION #2: Three Methods Of Learning

Three Learning Styles (from the Bepko Learning Center)

Everyone processes and learns new information in different ways. There are three main cognitive learning styles: Visual, Auditory, and Kinesthetic. The common characteristics of each learning style listed below can help you understand how you learn and what methods of learning best fits you. Understanding how you learn can help maximize time you spend studying by incorporating different techniques to custom fit various subjects, concepts, and learning objectives. Each preferred learning style has methods that fit the different ways an individual may learn best.

Common Characteristics

Visual
- Uses visual objects such as graphs, charts, pictures, and seeing information
- Can read body language well and has a good perception of aesthetics
- Able to memorize and recall various information
- Tends to remember things that are written down
- Learns better in lectures by watching them

Auditory
- Retains information through hearing and speaking

- Often prefers to be told how to do things and then summarizes the main points out loud to help with memorization
- Notices different aspects of speaking
- Often has talents in music and may concentrate better with soft music playing in the background

Kinesthetic
- Likes to use the hands-on approach to learn new material
- Is generally good in math and science
- Would rather demonstrate how to do something rather than verbally explain it
- Usually prefers group work more than others

In other words:

Visual – You can read about it.

Auditory – You can talk to others and learn from their experience with it.

Kinesthetic – You can pee on the electric fence to find out for yourself.

The purpose of this book is to let you take notes during the lecture portion of the School I will be presenting. It gives you something to read along while I talk to you about this industry "The Business of Being Santa". I will be sharing information I have learned by the three methods listed above and passing them along to you in both the first and second modes in the hopes you avoid the third method and the consequences thereof.

For those of you that decide to experiment with the Kinesthetic after the completion of this course, I reserve the right to point and laugh. Listen to what I have to say, read this book and ask questions, lots and lots of questions.

The finest school of higher learning is a log with a student on one end and an instructor on the other.

SECTION #3: The Evolution Of The Santa Image

St Nicholas was a real living person of history that was documented in record. Many of his actions and deeds are the basis of our Christmas traditions. From St Nicholas' time to the late 1700's there were numerous traditions with a central figure based upon St Nicholas and each had very special stories and traditions linked to that character. Father Christmas, Father Winter, Grandfather Frost, Sinter Claus and many, many more.

In the 1700's and early 1800's many people immigrated to America and they brought their traditions with them. As they generally celebrated at Christmas time and the Winter Solstice, they would invite their friends and neighbors to join in their celebrations. Thus the various traditions were blended and mixed.

The Knickerbocker Papers were the first written mention of a character that resembles the modern day Santa. Then after several other publications followed suit, Clement C. Moore wrote his poem "A visit from St. Nicholas" in 1822. No one remembered the name of the story, they referred to it by the first line "Twas the Night Before Christmas" and that firmly "fixed" the image of the modern day Santa since that time on.

The image was further defined and refined first by Thomas Nast, 1872 and then further by Haddon Hubbard "Sunny" Sundblom (June 22, 1899 – March 10, 1976) an artist best known for the images of Santa Claus he created for The Coca-Cola Company.

While based upon the various traditions of St Nicholas from many countries, "Santa Claus" is and remains a totally American invention and is now being exported to the rest of the world. Santa has been used advertise products ranging from cigarettes, pipes & tobacco to shaving items to watches & jewelry to food stuff & soda pop to vehicles. Santa has also been promoted supporting the troops during times at war dating back to the American Civil War through the Vietnam conflict all the way through to today's deployments of troops in foreign lands. Santa has promoted all manner of commercial item and has been sitting in stores and malls to listen to the wishes and desires of Children of all ages.

While "Santa" may have started out as an advertising tool in the later part of the 1860's through to today, the image and character of Santa is still changing and maturing along with the traditions surrounding his appearance. Many movies being made in the last century and the last 14 years have added to this change in traditions and are part of why the traditions surrounding Santa have changed so rapidly in comparison to those that formed in the "Old World". Several titles come to mind. Miracle on 34th Street (1947), Santa Claus (1959), Santa Claus Conquers the Martians (1964), A Christmas Story (1983), Santa Claus: The Movie (1985), The Santa Clause (1994) and Jingle All The Way (1996), just to name a few spanning the last 80 years.

The most prominent shift from "Old World" to "New" is the basic concept of a visit from Santa. Father Christmas, Father Winter, Grandfather Frost was more in the idea of bringing "judgment". To good children he brought candy, nuts, fruit, a few coins and perhaps a small gift or two usually left on the table, in a stocking or shoe. The bad children received lumps of coal, a raw potato, pickled egg and perhaps a bundle of twigs or sticks known as a "faggot" usually used to start a fire. This practice of "judgment" varied from country to country as did St Nicholas' mode of transportation and companions.

The tradition of Santa has always been one of a gift giver of love and forgiveness. This tradition has roots in the St Nicholas traditions but has become a focus of the character in main part.

Lately in the last 15 years a movement to shift the concept of "Santa" towards that of a more "Old World" tradition of St. Nicholas has been becoming a popular concept for those more interested in the deeper religious influences while others are striving to make their presentation based upon the drawing of Nast including the "Stars & Bars" Santa that was drawn to promote the Union effort in the War between the States. The inclusion of religious crosses and the influence of the Sundblom "Coca Cola" Santa suit have also been added to the mix.

Santa was once a character used to celebrate the season generally starting to make his appearance from Black Friday through New Year's Day. Now Santa is involved in Malls starting as early as October, seen in amusement parks year round and increasingly involved in "Care & Comfort" visits year round to disaster locations in the United States. The "Convoy of Toys" started by the Lone Star Santa group has influenced several other groups to start their own programs of a similar nature. Santa America has been working with hospice groups providing Santa visits year round for about a decade now. All of these activities are a distinct break from Father Christmas sitting in his Grotto waiting for visitors.

The image of Santa is changing constantly as the role is expanded to meet new challenges. It will remain an "Image in Flux" as long as new interpretations and traditions continue to be developed. As recent developments have shown, while the image of the "Home Visit Santa" and the definition of the "Mall Santa" have pretty much jelled, the total concept of "Santa" has yet to be reached and there will be new ideas, new concepts and images and "jobs" for Santa coming in the future. In a very real sense of the word, Santa is what you make of him for some time to come.

SECTION #4: The Future Of Being Santa

As for the future, everyone has an opinion and the crystal ball is always cloudy. I can share with you some of the trends I have watched over the last 33 years in the business.

If you take a trip in the "Way Back Machine" and land in 1982 you would see a much different business model that today! No one had to undergo a background check unless you were working with a government contract and even then it was exceedingly rare that "Santa" would have to be subjected to this. Drug testing and insurance for performers was an even rarer requirement to come across.

The Santa World was one very much like the Magician's World. Not a lot of publicity for the genre but you would see stories about "Santa's arrival" in just about every paper and on a few news programs starting about the week before Thanksgiving. There was "Santa's Village" and occasionally you would see a piece on "Santa in the Summer" but for the most part this was a job that Santas did 4-6 weeks out of the year and then they went about their lives until it was time to put the suit on again the following year.

Santa Schools were not very well publicized and most of them were focused on Mall work or the Salvation Army. This is a personal recollection and others perceptions may vary from mine due to their locality but in So Cal, this was the norm.

By 1992 Santa had become a popular (very busy) venue for such entertainment companies as Eastern Onion and other Singing Telegram companies across the country. You would see advertising to the public to have "Santa" come and visit YOUR home! The middle class started to host more and bigger Christmas Parties featuring a visit and gift giving by Santa. So too, marketing using more photos of "Santa" to decorate the catalogs and commercials on television became more prevalent. The venue was growing larger and faster than ever before.

Then in 1994 there was a photo shoot for a German catalog that was done in So Cal., and 12 Santas were hired to do this. After the shoot they had lunch and decided to make it an annual social thing, sort of a "tongue in cheek" kind of joke. Each year they came together to break bread and share their worst kid stories. Funny thing is, they had more people show each year than the last and pretty soon they started to generate "human interest" stories simply by being an eccentric group of bearded gentlemen that gathered once a year and shared the common interest of being Santa. Also beginning at this time, background checks and insurance to protect Malls and Corporations became a more common requirement, partly due to news stories that exposed "Bad" Santas sitting in those chairs. That was also around the time some companies started requiring drug testing as a requirement for employment.

Now during the years between 1983 and 1994 I ran into perhaps 25 Santas working the same area venues I did and I covered about 4 counties spanning over 27000 sq. miles. To be sure I did not know or meet every Santa that worked in So Cal, but I did meet most of the ones that worked for the same 17 entertainment companies I worked for. My exposure was to "Home Visit" Santas more than Mall or Photo advertising Santas. Then In 2000 I noticed an upsurge in the number of Santas working the same venues. In 1990 I was 35 yrs. old and very busy as a home visit Traditional Santa. In 2000 I was 45 and very busy as a RB Santa but the Santas I was working with or meeting were changing. I had been involved in a small way with IUSC from the beginning with the very first one at USC. I was seeing the last of the WW2 generation coming into the Santa World and the very first waves of the Baby Boomer generation starting to become Santa. It was an exciting time for Santas because we were becoming more communicative and forming groups and clubs. Something that had been kept very quiet up until then was becoming recognized as a viable consideration in the business of the season. Santas were able to learn how to negotiate contracts and what to ask for. They were taught what to do and what to avoid while interacting with the public in larger and larger groups. Better products and custom made items became easier to find and purchase. The level of professionalism rose sharply. So too did the numbers of working Santa.

Jump forward to 2006 and you see a professional Santa organization that had members numbering over 800, with members from around the world. You also see the first Discover Santa convention that was held in Branson with over 301 Santas in attendance in early July! This was pretty much unprecedented in the history of American Santa. The Bakken was bigger but few had heard of the Bakken inside the Santa circles here. Here we see the first mention and appearances by many of the current "big" names in the Santa World: Nicholas Trolli, Cindylu Thomas, Joe Moore, Ric Erwin, and Bob Callahan to name a few. Most of those mentioned were relatively new to the Santa World at that time but they made up for lost time shortly after the 2006 Branson event was done. On the way back from Branson to Southern California, the radio stations were all talking about the "Santa Convention" that had just happened in Branson. Every time we stopped to get gas, people would ask us if we had been a part of that event and wanted to take pictures of us. From 2006 to 2007 the membership of that little group went from around 800 to almost 1400.

As in everything, when you have enough people gathered together to spend their time and money on a business/hobby/shared interest there will be people that want to place themselves into that money stream and so we saw a proliferation of belt makers, suit makers, buckle makers, button makers and after 2006, event planners aimed toward gathering groups of Santa together to share their experience with others while buying or selling specialized products marketed toward the Santa market. Some did a decent or even outstanding job of doing so and made a decent profit in the process. Others ended up on the front page of the WSJ above the fold, or brought into court by the Cities and vendors they neglected to pay. All the while, more and more Santas were coming into the world sharing a smaller and smaller piece of the pie. There are some 4000 + malls that hire Santa in the US last time I checked a few years ago. There are many more than 4000 Santas out there currently and the number is still growing.

Now we look into the misty future. The Baby Boomer generation is right now hitting retirement age in greater numbers than ever before. The crest is yet to hit but it will in the next 5 years. This means even more Santa trying to compete for those jobs out there. Coupled to a recession of length and depth that has not been seen in 50 years, we have people that are looking to supplement their income any way they can. Can't blame them. When the supply of a service or product exceeds the demand for same, prices drop. It becomes a buyer's market and we see a drop in money paid to Santa simply because there are more options to the person hiring than before. This in turn will have some Santas retiring or dropping out from working in this business, especially those that think money matters most. When you turn your nose up at an offering of $X amount some other fellow is going to say $X is way better that $0 and take the job. No amount of complaining about "the good old days" or accusing the hired "HR" person the company prefers to filter their hired help through will change that. There is no Santa Union that will call for a strike. There are only market forces in play.

Now what does this mean to the average Santa? Well it lets you make some choices now about how to face the future challenges. The past model is gone and dead. You must make yourself more attractive to those that are offering the position/job/money than your competitor. Skills and talents that will make you more versatile and employable would include but not be limited to being fluent in more than one language, know sign language, have musical skills such as playing an instrument or being able to sing, having story telling skills, acting skills and oratory skills down to practicing good hygiene including being able to stop smoking during season and having a full set of teeth. The people that are hiring are looking at more than just the suit and how you fill it out. They want you to be able to pass a full 50 state background check, have insurance above a certain amount (in many cases in excess of $3 million in liability WITH a $500,000 child molestation rider), and pass a drug test while maintaining your overall health. The bar keeps getting set higher while the competition keeps growing. How you deal with this is up to you.

Everything goes in cycles. There are long cycles and short ones. The oldest Santas are now going to be falling out of the competition due to age, injury and illness. That is part of the cycle. The influx of new Santas has more than compensated for this attrition resulting in the supply having met or even exceeded the demand for the service. Think of ways to make yourself stand out in the crowd so that you are the one they want to hire to be "Their" Santa. This cycle is going to be longer than most so if you're going to be Santa, find a way to make it enjoyable for you as you go down this path.

SECTION #5: The Secret of Life!

Hello all you fellow Wish granters, Dream enablers and all around nice people. I wish to expound upon the true "Secret" of life and how it can change your entire outlook on how you approach life and others in it.

First let me ask you a question and before you read further, try to answer it as honestly and truthfully as you can, if only to yourself.

The question is, "What do you want to be in Life?" another way of asking the question is "What do you want out of Life?"

It is a simple question and I will give you the answer a little further down but for now take the time and write down your answer on a piece of paper for later reference.

OK, Got your answer written down? Good! Let us continue with revealing the "Secret" of Life!

No peeking until you wrote down your answer!

The "Secret" of life is to be happy. To be happy you must find what makes you happy and pursue that activity with passion. I was in my first orientation class in college when I was asked that question along with about 40 other bright young people and our answers were things like "a house", "a car" or "a big pile of money", some of us wanted to have "a family" or "a career" but no one truly answered the question. The answer is to be reasonably happy. Find something that makes you reasonably happy and then find a way to get paid to do it.

I have worked in a career, Union man in a construction field of endeavor. Became a Millwright in a lumber mill and while the work was interesting, varied and paid fairly well, it was work and not fun. Towards the end of my time there I found ways to make it fun at times but mostly it was just work. Show up every morning and punch in, work to quitting time to punch out and live for the weekends. I was married and supporting my wife as best I could in every way I could, but I was rarely ever happy.

Then I had the opportunity to escape that and by chance I learned to be happy once again. I enjoy the freedom to do as I please and I please to do what I do. I work as an entertainer. Not everybody would be happy doing this. Some folks love baking cakes. Others really have fun driving across the country. Still others enjoy drinking beer. The trick is to find a way to get paid to do what you enjoy doing! THAT is the "Secret" of life! I have met people that get paid to eat Ice Cream. I know a couple of guys that get paid to ride roller coasters. One fellow I met gets paid to drive from city to city in a truck and for him it is the greatest thing in the world. Siskel and Ebert got paid to watch movies and critique them.

Candy tasters. Cookie makers. Toy makers. It does not matter what you do in life as long as you are the very best that you can be and enjoy doing it! Then your work is your play and it really is interesting how little money it takes to be happy.

Working at a job for money is not the path to happiness. Nobody wants to do something they can't stand for any amount of money. You will quickly quit and look for other employment rather that do something you hate if all you are doing it for is money. Or you stay in it and stay very unhappy in life. You can have multiple careers in your life! Doing the some thing you hate every day for 30 years is like "hard labor" and few people do that voluntarily. Usually they do it while wearing an orange jump suit breaking rocks as a guest of the penal system.

Find what makes you happy and find a way to support yourself doing it. I go to people's homes and make them laugh. I fire their imaginations and get them to forget the impossible for a short time. I bring a little surreal into their lives. And at the end of the hour, I go on to another party. I have done this for 31 years now and though I do not have a 401k or benefits, I am happy and never plan to retire from what I do. I plan on and will continue to entertain as long as I have a means to communicate with my audience. Once that is no longer an option, my time here on this world will come to an end but I will be happy even then knowing I did a good job and the children I visited that grew up to have children of their own and had me visit them and those children have grown up and now I am visiting their children with the same fun and wonder. Be it as a Magician, a Balloon twister, a Face Painter, a Story teller or Santa, they will remember that time we spent together and feel happy once again.

Find your "Secret" and hold on to it with all you passion! Build it and develop it into being the best anyone has ever seen. Be memorable and most of all have fun!

SECTION #6: A Topic That No One Wants To Approach

One way of looking at it is:
""Naughty" Joke To Adults Gets Beloved Macy's Santa Fired"
Or another headline on the same story:
"Bad Santa Fired From Macy's Over Lewd Joke | The Stir"

Two different headlines on the same story. This happened back in 2010 and was perhaps a bit of an overreaction on the part of the adults involved (No children were present or privy to the joke telling) and also of that on the part of Macy's but it is a problem that is growing.

The Santa involved with the first example was John Toomey who told a joke to an adult couple that had asked, "Why are you always smiling?" His reply was "I know where all the naughty girls and boys live." Macy's pulled John out of the chair before the next break. No hesitation on the part of the employer to get that Santa out of their building once they had a customer complaint. This is after working the same location for 20 years.

John appeared on the Tonight Show and shared his story. He was later hired by the Pub "Lefty O'Doul's", where John collected over 10,000 toys for the children of his city and also earned much more money than he ever did working for Macy's – a small silver lining. Sadly John Toomey passed away in July of 2011 at age 69.

In 2013 we had:
"Man arrested, banned from playing Santa, after Hanover Mall incident"

"Herbert Jones, 62, now faces indecent assault and battery after cops say he got handsy with Santa's Little Helper, leaving the teen in tears as she recounted what had happened to detectives, The Smoking Gun reports.

Read more: http://www.nydailynews.com/news/crime/mall-santa-62-molested-female-teen-elf-barred-playing-st-nick-cops-article-1.1528938#ixzz2rrfvusVu"

Even if he did not do what he is accused of he has to fight the case in court, then find a new venue to perform in and on top of that, has lost an entire season over what was possibly a bad act of judgment.

Another: "Winterport lawmaker fired as Bangor Mall Santa after saying 'I don't give a damn'"

Joe Brooks, who had been working as Santa six days a week since Nov. 15, said he was very upset when he was fired by two female representatives of Noerr Programs Inc., which operates a shopping center photo services nationwide.

Joe recalled the evening they called him during his break:

At about 6:00 pm I got a phone call from corporate headquarters in Colorado. Two women called me and said they were relieving me of my duties. When I asked them why, they said they were not going to tell me. I said this is a pretty serious matter, relieving Santa Claus five days before Christmas. They said, two weeks ago you were apprised of a complaint. This is a continuation of that. The four-time state representative, now an independent Santa said. They would not tell me what it [the complaint] was in reference too.

Brooks said the only thing that he can think of that could possibly have led to a complaint was a conversation he had with a staff member about three weeks ago during which he said, "I don't give a damn." Yes, I was in the kiosk and I probably should not have used that word, Brooks said. It was a private conversation. I didn't think twice about it.

What is the point of all of this? Simple. We need to become more aware of the things we say and the way we conduct ourselves in the public eye, especially in the High Volume Venue such as a Mall.

We are products of our upbringing and what was acceptable in the 70's and 80's as we grew into adult stature has become criminally actionable and socially unacceptable in the middle of the 2010 decade. As we have seen, the telling of an off color joke can now have major consequences. The act of touching anyone without his or her express permission is equally actionable. There is no such thing as a private conversation while you are dressed as Santa and in the public view at any time.

There is a reason for wearing white gloves while taking pictures. That is so your hands can be seen and you have proof you had not touched anyone inappropriately during the picture taking process.

Now we need to be just as aware of what we say and the context it is being said in if you wish to avoid the problems these recent cases have brought to light. At the least they can result in a reprimand all the way to losing your season and criminal prosecution.

Always remember you are there to bring Joy and Fun to those that visit with you. You having "fun" is not part of the job description. If you can not enjoy working this type of venue, then it is not for you and you should seek other venues to play the role of Santa such as home visit, corporate event or the new emerging Video Chat visit with Santa that has begun.

We live and work in a "One Way" environment. The customer can say ANYTHING they please on the set and there truly are no repercussions for them other than their possible removal of service and their being asked to leave the set by security. Certain actions and poses tried by customers will result in this but that varies from set to set and photo company to photo company. In the end, it is not so much what the customer does or says (provided the safety of the children is maintained and that of the set crew) it is what the public sees and hears from the Santa that is the issue.

This chapter addressed a growing problem in what the set Santa does and says and how the public receives it. Particularly by the individuals sitting on or interacting with Santa at any time Santa is in the public view. What show up in the papers are simply the more "sensational" examples that gain traction as a story to sell those papers. This also happens in private home visits and at corporate events as well but we rarely see those examples in the news simply because it isn't sensational enough to make it past the news editor. Upset a family visit or a couple of hundred people at a corporate party will not usually rise to the level of interest to make it to print.

This is not to say there are not repercussions. The agency that sends out that "problematical" Santa certainly hears about the problem, IN SPADES. For instance, the Santa that is one of several working a mall event over the course of several days (parachuting Santa, Tree lighting singing Santa and a couple of different Santa that cover the chair on different days) sits in the chair and does a wonderful job while in the public visit time but then walks over to his van and waves the one finger salute to several people as he drives off. The Santa that goes to an adult dinner party to sit for pictures a couple of hours and he spends much of his time flirting with the single ladies then peruses the buffet and eats without being invited to do so. Finally there is the Santa that calls the customer and says he cannot make it due to car trouble and in the background of the call the customer can hear the party and the host calling to Santa to come back to the chair for more pictures an hour and a half past his show up time for the customer he is calling.

These three examples are just a few I fielded behind the desk at the agency I was working at the time. In two of the instances it was the same Santa. I truly recommended using a different Santa after that second incident to the owner of the agency due to the loss of the customers and the refunds and difficulties that followed his actions. A fantastic looking Santa that works still to this day, but just not for that agency.

Our behavior and deportment is under extreme scrutiny at all times while in the suit and in the eye of the public. Certain behaviors that used to slide past as marginally acceptable have become actionable both criminally and civilly by law. It does not matter if the intent was to be humorous on the part of the Santa; we are not stand-up comedians doing a riff off of Don Rickles. Our performance is set by the public expectation and individual interpretation is not expected or always appreciated and can lead to repercussions from our arrival on scene to our departure. I am not speaking of actions or behaviors that someone does in their private life; I am only addressing those actions and words while in the public eye performing. Your performance is what you will be judged by in the public eye unless and until your actions privately brings you to the attention of the authorities and the press. That is a subject beyond the scope of this blog.

As with any of the chapters I have written, they have been meant to help educate or make you aware of existing or developing problems happening in the Business we all do when we play the role of Santa.

For those that say "Bah! I will say whatever I chose! It is a free country and I know how to be Santa!" this chapter is for you!

SECTION #7: What Separates A "Hobby" Santa From A Professional Santa?

To perform in any corporate setting such as a mall or any retail business, there is now a demand for insurance by the business you will be performing in/at. If you work for a photo company you will have to provide a background check as well. It is the way they do business and is in no way a comment upon you personally.

Just like auto insurance and registration for your car, Santa needs liability insurance and a background check. These two pieces of paper are part of what you need to have to perform as Santa in those environments. Depending on the company, you may have to provide them as you are an independent contractor dealing directly with the business, OR the photo company covers the expense for you with their coverage and does the background check as well. In this case these are only valid for working while employed by that company.

There was a time, 30 years ago, when you did not need these forms to perform as Santa but because of problems with child molesters, folks suing the business or mall because Santa did something inappropriate, and the possibility for injuries while handling small children, insurance is now demanded of those of us that want to perform in this arena. Don't want to take that step up into the mall or department store Santa leagues? You can still manage to get nice work doing private party work but if anything happens to dissatisfy the customer or one of the guests, you can still find yourself sued. Insurance relieves you of that worry.

There is far more to being Santa than answering the "call" and putting on the Red Suit when you enter the professional world of Santa. Even doing things for charitable events requires insurance and background checks these days. The two pieces of paper last for a year and then have to be renewed again to remain in force. Just like auto insurance and registration.

Along with this there are many other things that while not demanded for performing, should be looked at and considered as part of what you need to do every year to perform as Santa not only to protect the customer but to protect yourself as well just as insurance does.

SECTION #8: Being A Performer And A Santa

I am wondering how many of you are being Santa for what reasons? A recent thread on a web site has me curious as to motivations and desires of those involved with this endeavor being seen in public as Santa. I will list a few reasons why I know folks do this or what they say they are doing it for and then I will talk a little about the job itself beyond that. If you read this and have thoughts about what I write here, please respond here below and lay out your reason if I miss it.

Sample Reasons:

1. I feel that I portray Santa to serve the religious community in my area reminding them the true reason for the season.

1a. Only Christian children can come to sit on my lap! Santa has no service for or to any other denomination/belief system.

1b. It does not matter the faith or the person that comes to visit with me since I am in the character of Santa. All are welcome.

2. I enjoy performing as Santa bringing smiles to children of all ages.

3. I do the "Santa" thing because it is something to do during a season that is normally slow for me otherwise. It keeps me active.

3a. I wish to be recognized as the best/supreme Santa in my area viewed publicly as better than my peers and my advertising reflects this.

3b. I wish to be recognized as the superior Santa in a Group of Santas and make statements as such in my advertisements to my peers.

4. I am only in it for the money, as much as I can make.

4a. I am doing this to supplement my income/retirement so I wish to maximize my financial gain.

4b. The money is a secondary issue and as long as I get what I negotiated for it doesn't matter how much anyone else makes doing the same thing.

4c. I wish to be paid for what I bring to the Christmas season but money is not the overriding concern as long as I make enough to pay for the suit and upkeep.

5. I do this for free and donate any funds generated to charity.

5a. I only do this for charity.

5b. I do some charitable events at my choosing and try to make a profit the rest of the time.

6. I am a children's entertainer and this is one of the seasonal characters I perform as part of my business. I keep my prices in line with what I do year round.

6a. I am an entertainer and I charge as much as I can for limited premium time slots. If they want me they can pay through the nose on Christmas Eve!

6b. I keep my prices the same all the time. November 30th through December 25th, I get paid enough for what I do.

I am sure that there are many more reasons than what I have listed and many of you started with one reason or number of reasons and over time they have changed in direction or scope. Over the last 31 years, this has been the case for me and my journey down this path. Let me tell you about my getting here.

I was first Santa in the second grade in a school play. I was the fat kid and so cast in the part to play Santa. I had to walk down the center isle of the auditorium in my Santa suit and cotton beard throwing candy to the audience out of a white pillowcase "Santa" bag while the chorus sang "The Big Fat Man with the Long White Beard" over and over again. Mortifying to a fat kid in second grade! Simply hated the part and swore a 7 year old's oath to never have anything to do with Santa again!

At twelve, I developed an interest in magic, at eighteen I started to perform tricks for friends, and at twenty I did tricks to break the ice with pretty girls. I also sang in choir in school all the way through 12th grade and was active in sports. In 1980 I was involved in a motorcycle accident and during my rehab I became a clown and waived at cars in front of businesses. During that time my job in the lumber mill as a mill write disappeared and I stayed a clown to supplement my income while working retail. That winter 2 agencies asked me to do Santa for them and since clowning is slow in the winter, I said "sure". You could say I fell into being Santa after so long. I also did magic shows, company picnics, hospital visits and retirement homes along with convalescent care facility visits as any one of my various characters that Santa was just one of. At the peak of my time working for entertainment agencies I worked for seventeen of them at the same time along with working three weekday farmers markets as the street clown or street magician while working 40 hours a week in retail sales.

My first year as a Santa I did some 28 visits. I was a theatrical bearded Santa for the first 15 years until 1995. It was then I decided to grow my own beard out for a number of reasons. By 1995 I was making between 85 and 105 visits a season and theatrical bearded Santas were paid about $50 per visit by the agencies. I also had some 24 beard and wig sets that had to be cleaned and set each year and that cost me $20 each to have done. Real bearded Santas started out at $65 an hour and I only had to get my hair bleached out twice a season at $60 a pop! More money and less expense equal a great motivator to grow a beard! By '01 I had raised my price to the agencies to $100 an hour hoping to get less work and still make about the same amount of money. In 2000 I had done some 95 shows @ $85 an hour and the schedule was rather hectic. By '02 I was up to 115 shows a season and there I bounced between 115 and 130 shows per season until '08 when I started to sit in the mall. I worked weekdays, evening parties, weekends, 7 shows on Christmas Eve finishing up around 1 am and then getting up on Christmas Morning to be "caught" delivering presents starting at 5 am through to 9 am then did several Christmas night visits as well. The last Santa job for the season is New Year's Eve for Orthodox Greek parties. Now I work (if you can call it that) around 400 hours from the 11th of November through the 24th of December sitting in a comfortable chair and visiting with whoever comes by to sit on my knee in the mall. I still visit folk's homes on Christmas day but the price has remained pretty much the same for me as it was back in '07. I make enough and my performance is appreciated by the audience.

I hope to remain in the chair for at least the next 5-8 years before cutting back any further. Making the move to a mall environment was the same type of decision as going from wig and beard set to real beard. The overall money is comparable and yet there is far less wear and tear on my vehicle, suit and health. I also no longer have to pay for the hand out gifts like candy canes that I was going through at the rate of 8-10 cases a season. Since I see many of the same people every year in the mall, my sense of gratification and continuity is well satisfied as well.

So basically I started because it was a job that paid money during a traditionally slow time of the year originally and as my customer base grew I raised my prices to try to reduce my work load and when that didn't work out the way I had hoped, held to a strict "first come, first served" policy that saw me booking families in January for the following Christmas to ensure they got "their" Santa next season. If there was a scheduling conflict, folks were more than willing to shift the time or date of their party to accommodate my available schedule.

One family I visited every Christmas eve over the course of 26 years and I watched children grow up to become parents in their own right and they in turn introduced their children to "Santa" as well. It became a job that paid more money than it became a tradition and extended family and the money no longer was the overriding concern. I continue to work as Santa because it pleases me to do so and I do it very well and I am compensated well enough to make it worth my time and effort. It does not matter to me how much money anyone else makes doing the same kind of job I do.

On a side note, I like to network with other Santas and help them when I can. Many come into the shop looking to purchase their first "real" suit; others want to know what they should know before they begin. A few I have helped locally. Most notably is the Santa that works the Mission Inn (a local historical hotel and eatery where several movies have been filmed) credits me for his placement there, many of the local IE Santas have had help in work placement by my giving them the contact numbers and names to people that hire Santas, and one such example of my helping others is Sam S.

Sam came into the shop to look for western wear and some magic for his old west gunfighter character. As he had a nice beard, I asked him if he ever wore a red suit at Christmas time. Sam looked down at me and sneered, "Do I look like the kind of fella that would have children sit on his knee?" Taken aback I apologized saying it was a way to make a little money in what is an off-season for most performers. Sam's entire demeanor change and he asked "Money? Tell me more!" I gave him some advice, pointed him towards a good suit maker in the area, gave him the name and number of some people that could help him find work and now Sam has become the #1 Santa for the Amuse Matte Company.

SECTION #9: Negotiations And The Business Of Being Santa

February and the last season has been put to bed. Our equipment is being refurbished and renewed. Our suits are being cleaned and repaired. New materials and accessories are being purchased in anticipation of the next season that will start in about 8 months from now.

None of this is new. What is new is a number of Santas that have had their first taste of working in a mall situation. For them it was a mixed bag review of good/bad experiences and we now see and hear some of the complaints about the way they were treated when working these venues. As I have pointed out in the past year and a half, the Baby Boom generation has hit the Santa work force in massive numbers and they are running into situations they never considered before.

Part of this is due to assumptions and expectations made by those that approached this business as a "Warm and Fuzzy" type of "people will treat me fairly because I am Santa" kind of mind set. It does not matter what their background or work experience or education has been, this seems to cut across all levels and it seems to mostly (but not always or exclusively) affect real beard Santas. I really hate to burst anyone's "Warm and Fuzzy" Bubble but when you perform as Santa or as any type of entertainer, you are working as an Independent Contractor and are treated much like a commodity whose services are bought, repackaged and sold again.

Now before you say "I do not work for anyone else, I book all my own shows!" you are simply acting as your own agent and selling your service to the customer direct in competition with everyone else in the business. Yes you have a bit more control over your presentation/performance that way but in the end you have to please the customer and that is the bottom line.

The problem seems to stem from a lack of attention to detail when negotiating the contract. The unhappy stories all seem to reflect this no matter if you're working for an agency, a photo company or for yourself. So I would say:

Negotiation is the Name of the Game!

Working as Santa has a LOT in common with Professional Sports. You have your new guys, rookies just starting out and they play for the love of the game. Some are outstanding and some need a little polish before they are ready to move up. Then there are those that have little talent or ability but love the sport so much they simply keep trying to be "in the game" no matter how.

Just like in Professional Sports, Professional Santas move from the "Home Visit" venue to the "larger event" venue when they have enough experience and are more comfortable in the larger scope of performance. Sort of like going from High School/College athletics into a Farm League team. From there you go into AA and Pro League Teams.

In Santa terms that could mean going from doing it for free for your family, at a local charity and church functions to doing it for pay in home visits and corporate parties to (in the Pro League) doing it for Mall venues and television/movie production.

Big time Ball players get to be paid well for something they love to do and do well. The same thing holds true for Professional Santas. You get paid for something you do that you would do for charity. The main problems stem from perceived mistreatment of the performer (assumptions not being met) and (sometimes) the ego of the performer (Expectations of treatment and status).

Take a page from the big time sports page. Learn to play the "Game". I am not talking about the performance, but the negotiations that occur before you even pull on the suit and boots. No matter what level of Santa you are, you will have to negotiate before the performance. For a charity or for a home visit to working in a mall or shooting video work you will be involved in some form of negotiation.

- What time is the event to start?
- How long will I be there?
- Where is it going to be?
- What will be expected of me EXACTLY?
- What will I be expected to provide?
- What will the venue be expected to provide?
- What will be the compensation?
- Will there be a "green/dressing/break room made available?

- Will there be ONLY red and green M&Ms in my snack bowl?
- If you are working out of state, specify that you are to be placed in a hotel/motel that meets a minimum of quality (does not rent by the hour) and serves a breakfast in the morning.
- If you are commuting to and from over long distance (over 30 miles each way daily), make sure there is a "Travel allowance" included in the contract.

All this and more apply equally to Pro Sports and being Santa!

If you are going to be a professional Santa Claus, take the time and make the effort to do the job as a professional. For once you sign that contract, your bed is made and you must sleep in it for the duration of the terms or pay the consequences of the penalties listed within the contract. Too many times I have seen or heard of people being pulled into court over a failure to adhere to and provide the terms of an entertainment contract. All it takes is for the end customer to "perceive" a loss of service or value from their contracted entertainment.

In the case of Mall work, you really have to nail down the details in the contract before you sign. The reason for this is there is usually a "Third Party" involved with the ability to alter the terms of the contract if they are not spelled out. That "Third Party" is the mall itself. Before you sign the contract which states "hours of performance will be from set open to set close", you might want to nail down those hours of operation first. Otherwise the set hours are what the mall says they are, any time during the run of the contract. Sometimes they will try and run a line that reads "You are required to remain in the chair and on the set until the last person in line at close of set has had the chance to visit and get the picture." and they will frame that clause as a possibility of being used anytime during the last 2 weeks of the contract run. Even if you get your hours nailed down the "Third Party" has the right to alter the hours as "needed".

You are working as a contract employee and not as an hourly rate, which means you will be working longer hours than you anticipated. One way for you to address this is while your negotiating the terms of the contract, simply write in that your hours are as stated in the contract and if the hours are extended, you are to be paid $xx.xx per hour not covered under the base agreement. So you start out working a 375 -400 hour contract and over the last 16 days they extend the hours by 3 hours a day by opening the set an hour early and closing the set 2 hours later due to the Mall wanting to accommodate the crowds, you would receive 48 hours of overtime pay at the rate you contracted for instead of getting nothing more than the base pay you signed up for. That is a week's pay extra on a 6-week contract. Of course that may be a deal breaker and the Photo Company might just go find a new guy to do the job.

Negotiation is just as important to your having a good time in the chair as any other pre-season preparation you do. If you sign a contract without understanding it with the expectation that you will be treated fairly simply because you are Santa, you will eventually (sooner not later) be disappointed with your experience.

After all, Being Santa is just about the BEST job in the world! Satisfaction comes from paying attention to all the little details. Take the time and make the effort to look into the details before doing any job or signing any contract. You will then only have to worry about being Santa and having fun doing it. My only other advice to you once you sign the contract is to keep your hands and feet inside the ride until it comes to a complete stop at the end of the season.

SECTION #10: Pricing Your Services

The very first thing you hear spoken out of the mouth of any new performer is "How much do you charge?" Meaning, how much can I get? Well folks, it varies wildly and widely from performer to performer and geographical location. Here are some words of advice which you are free to use or ignore as that is what it cost you to receive.

First you must determine "**how much**" you want in return for your efforts and time. To do this you take all the expenses you would incur while engaged in the activity such as transportation to and from the event, the consumables used in doing the job such as the giveaways you hand out and the meal you ate on the road along with the fuel you burned to travel to and from the show. These are basic costs of operation per show. Set this total aside for later use. If the show is out of your area to travel in a reasonable length of time you have to factor in the cost of the lodging as well.

Now you factor in the wear and tear on your suit and equipment and upon your health. You take the cost of your equipment such as the suit, boots, belt, bag and any props or accessories you use in the performance of your show. This includes doctor visits, dry cleaning, make up and boot polish among many other items. You take that total and divide it by the number of shows you will be doing to get a "per performance" cost approximation. Add this to the total from the first paragraph. A good suit will last you at least 5 years and hopefully 8-10 years as will a quality pair of boots and anything else that is of a quality nature. You need to determine the number of performances you will be willing to do per season and use that as your divider, you can work more but have a target number of shows that you want to limit yourself to do to make back enough to pay for the costs. I picked 90 as my target number originally. So a way to factor the cost per show for replacing the suit is like this:

Suit cost $500.00 divided by 5 years = $100. Divide by 90 shows per year = $1.12 per show rounded up but that is just the replacement cost of the suit. You still have to factor in all the other costs as well. Since I have a policy of buying and having multiple suits for back up and rotation my actual operation costs for just suits is closer to this formula. New suit every 4 years with a life expectancy of 7-8 years of use and an overlap factor of 3 at any time runs something like $2.08 per performance cost. Having multiple suits will lower the wear and tear on the individual suit, extending the life expectancy of each suit to over 8 years and that makes for economy of scale and lowers the overall cost. By the end of any 8 year period on a suit I have usually donated the suit in good condition to someone starting out.

Now you figure what your time is worth by taking a figure you want to earn in total for the season and dividing it by the number of shows you are willing to do. Let's say you want to make a total of $10,000.00 a season working only from Black Friday to December 23. That will mean you work only a total of 24 days in the year 2012, as Dec 1st is the Saturday after Black Friday next year. You will have exactly 8 weekend days for your prime party dates with 4 Fridays thrown in if you work Black Friday for a total of 12 days of work unless you book week days as well. Let further suppose you work 4 parties a day on all Saturdays and Sundays with 2 parties on Fridays for a total of 40 parties. Hmmmm... That falls well short of the 90 shows per season target. I guess that means you either have a higher per event cost expense or you book more shows during the week and weekend. I usually worked as many as 10 -12 shows a weekend and 2 to 4 a week day during season but on the shortest season of the cycle which is 2012 coming up, I was real lucky to work 90 events in a short season. Anyway let's say you did your 90 target number for the season that would be $10,000.00 divided by 90 = $112.00 rounded up. Subtract the cost of incidentals such as Candy Canes @ $3.00 a dozen (way cheaper when you buy them by the gross lot case.), your $2.00 suit replacement costs, your transport costs, your insurance costs, your other job costs that vary from job to job and you don't have much. So you add $32 to each show to bring the cost to the consumer up to $150 per visit. But the other guy in your market area is charging @200 an hour and you don't want to undercut the market so you raise your price to $200.00 an hour! There! That should do it! But wait, I only am doing 40 parties maybe next year unless I really work it hard so that only makes me $8000.00 for the season! Arrgh! Raise the price again! Gotta make that money! I know! Charge triple on Christmas Eve, the night we celebrate the reason for the season and even more on Christmas day! Then I make the amount I need to be happy! Is it just me or is the cost of doing business getting a bit foggy? Let's wipe the board clean and make it simple.

You set your price and stick to it. As long as you get what you need to be happy performing as Santa, it does not matter what someone else is making. I see so many new Santas saying "It is all about the children" and in the next breath saying they are not getting enough bookings to make it worthwhile. Nobody can tell you what to charge, as that is what you have to decide for yourself. What do you need to do the job? Now add a little bit more to that for your profit margin. Retail sales are usually figured to produce a margin of 40% to 60% markup. Maybe that would work for you too. If it costs you $40 dollars to perform the show, charge $100 and make

60% profit for your trouble. If you feel your worth more than that, charge more.

If your price is lower than the rest of your competition and your quality is equal in all respects, you will command a greater share of the market. If you raise your price higher than your local market is willing to pay, you will garner less of that market than your competition. This is called market forces of supply and demand. The higher the quality and value you offer for your service, the greater your demand will be and the greater the price you can command for your service.

Charge whatever you feel your time is worth by setting your own price. If it is too high they will simply reject your offer. If it is too low you will simply be busy working for what you asked for. By asking what others negotiate you do 3 things. You set your value by other people's yardstick. You set up a situation of "Price Fixing". You limit your satisfaction in doing a job due to setting your expectations based upon others responses.

By setting your worth by what others make you are ignoring many factors. Do you wish to be placed in a mall in another state? The people you perceive as making more may be working in a better economic area that where you live. Better economies mean they can afford to pay higher wages for qualified professionals. This is true in any vocation. Do you have special talents? Storytelling, musical talent, dance, magic, acting credentials and/or stagecraft? These have value in the negotiations as well but only if the company and mall is seeking them. Do you wish to work within 10, 25 or 90 miles from your home? Will you want to be compensated for your travel or do you want to be provided with a rental vehicle? If staying in a hotel/motel provided by the contracting company, do you want to be fed as well? This is all part of the fee you are negotiating.

Sit down and figure out what you feel your time is worth to you and then you have found your rate. Your experience and talents are what you bring to the table as well as your "look" and personality. When you're negotiating a Mall contract, you are not doing a "daily rate" but a total fee for the run of the contract. That is what you are working with. To get the "daily rate" you then divide the total amount of the contract by the number of days it runs. Contracts can run from 32 days to 60. Hours per day will vary. Many people try to get a "Number of hours" and apply an hourly rate to that to achieve the contract amount. This is done in negotiation with the representative of the company you wish to work for.

Do you wish to work for $15 an hour? $20? $25? $30? $50? Do you want to work 300 hours? 400? 12 hours a day or 7-8? This is what you need to consider along with travel expenses and housing costs as well as cleaning, repair and replacement of your suit and equipment. That bottom line number is different for everyone.

By sitting down and doing the computations of your own worth, you will find greater satisfaction in doing the event/contract. You will get what you feel is your worth for your efforts and it does not matter what anyone else earns as long as you are satisfied with your payment. Price yourself too low and you will be very busy. Price yourself too high and you can price yourself right out of a market.

I sit in a mall now and I am paid enough to compensate me for my efforts and still allow me to be Santa. I no longer compete in the open market of home visit but when I did I was working anywhere from 95 shows a short cycle year to over 135 shows a season @ $100 an hr. with mileage paid for anything over 25 miles in any direction and tips were very nice, especially on

Christmas Eve and Christmas Day. Many times equaling more than the hourly rate earned.

After all is said and done, I take home more now than I ever did even on my best season due to the elimination of many costs incurred by travel and giveaways. It is a good way to be Santa but not for everybody. You must find your own path to follow.

Be Santa for the children and share the message of Joy, Peace and Hope for the future.

SECTION #11: Outsource HR/Placement Agencies And How They Can Work For You

Businesses such as Babies R Us, Bass Pro Shops, Cabellas, Macy's, Petco, Sears, Walmart and other High Volume Vendors (HVV) look to Outsource HR/Placement Agents like Cindy Claus of Party Palz, Gina Bacon of Nationwide Santas, Tim Connaghan of the Kringle Groups, Carmen Tellez of CharmandHappy, Roz Watson of Hire a Santa out of Canada along with many others to fill those chairs. In all cases the outsourced HR/placement agent is the intermediary point of contact between the location/store manager and the performer.

The Businesses hiring are using the seasonal icon of a "live" Santa as a "Draw" to bring customers into their stores. They offer low cost or free "Pictures with Santa" as a way to increase seasonal traffic into their locations. Since it is a low cost or free operation, the HVV using the performer (Santa) is in search for the highest Quality (Insured, reliable, drug screened and background checked) for the lowest possible price. Basically these are entry-level positions for such types of venue. These types of locations can be Statewide, Regional wide, Nationwide or even International in scope.

In just about each case, the outsourced HR/placement agent funnels the prospective performers to the location managers who then make the final selection of who will sit in the chair at each location. In many situations, the HVV will wish to "Hot Seat" the chair using 2 or even 3 shifts of performers to limit the time in the chair and reduce fatigue and stress on the performer while keeping the line moving without breaks.

Quite often you will hear of one Santa or another complains about the "Deal" they got through such a placement agent. They feel they were not treated well by the location and somehow this was the fault of the person that fed them into the placement process and interview with the location manager. That actually is on the performer as the negotiations of the contract is such the performer must be aware of the particulars before agreeing to the job. This will be addressed in a different section of this book.

The agent is the intermediary point of contact between the HVV and the Santa hired to sit in the chair. The HVV does not wish to handle the scheduling or the individual problems a Santa might encounter such as illness or personal problems. That is also part of the agent's job. Think of the agent as an outsourced HR dept.

I will not say what the agent is paid to do this but I will say it is far less than many suppose. From the agent's portion of what is their compensation they pay the travel and housing for those Santas working away from their home. They also pay for the replacement Santa when one of the Santas already placed cannot do the job. Their hours are not 6 hour shifts but more like 14 to 16 hours a day riding herd on a group of eclectic but talented individuals.

Part of the equation (and sometimes cause for gripes) is the total amount paid in the contract. $25 an hour is not below what a lot of malls pay. It is the number of hours worked that determines you total contract. Four hour shift hot seating means $100 a day worked or $5000 for a 200 hour standard contract. This is the biggest bone of contention for most "old hand" Santas. This is governed by how many days HVV wants to run their promotion and how many of those days are running at full time capacity. The home office sets that with small deviations on the local manager's initiative. The agent that places you has no control over that.

Now the more Santas an agent places, the more that agent earns per season but the amount per Santa is much lower than many think. A lot of Santas believe they are "professional" because they have been through 2 or 5 or 7 years of seasonal performance and may have attended a few 1 or 2 or 4 day schools. In our business, that would be the norm for such a claim and accepted as such.

I hope this shades the opinion some Santas seem to have about agents in general. Do not misconstrue my writings as defending outsourced HR/placement agents.

In general it seems that agents are viewed as a necessary evil at best at times. But to sit in 90%+ of malls or mall like situations you need to deal with a placement officer or agent that represents one of the photo companies or an entertainment company such as Nationwide Santas or Party Palz or any number of other such.

I gave this information to give the members of IBRBS as well as others an insight into what is going on behind the scenes they may not be totally aware of and some background on the one of the people that facilitates the introduction of individual Santas to the Chair they sit in.

It is a common reaction to blame change on the person that works with and around the change that affects your situation. The reason for change is not that person adapting to the situation but forces both economic and policy on the part of the job creator such as the mall or the business hiring the Santa.

The days of negotiating with the HVV company on an individual basis have mostly passed and those Santas that are enjoying a higher wage working for them currently are working under contracts that were finalized before the change in policy and once they run their course and expire, those seats will be filled under the current policy and restrictions. It is time now to look at the playing field and decide what you are interested in doing as a working Santa performer. The one constant unchanging thing in the entertainment business is, nothing stays the same. The economy and the wishes of those that hire are constantly in flux and shifting. We as performers have to watch and take advantage of the changes as best we can.

Do not become welded to a particular way of thinking when doing business. Your business model will eventually (and probably sooner than you think), become inoperative in the changing times. Gina shifted her agency business from local (countywide) to regional (statewide) to now nationwide representing of varied talent. That also means she accepts and attempts to fill job requests from all across the country and beyond, in some cases. Most of us only focus on what is in our immediate viewpoint and do not look at the big picture of change. In doing so we cut ourselves off from possibilities and tend to blame those that "take advantage" of us. If you are going to be "professional" you need to be aware of the changes in our industry across the board, not just in our own location or circumstance.

If you decide to work for one of the larger Photo Companies you will be Negotiating with the person that hires the talent for that company, be it Cherry Hill, Noerr, AmuseMatte, Sepia, Picture People or any other such company. These Talent scouts are looking to make the best deal they can for their company. And while they will honor what is written in it, they will not go out of their way to make sure you understand completely what is involved. There are exceptions and companies have been making an effort to be more "upfront" and informative over the last few years because Malls like to have the same Santa working each year for continuity and customer draw. Things have gotten better with working out contracts and Santas have started to learn how to ask for what they need to have to make a contract comfortable to work under.

The more you know, the better you can make choices and decisions. Remember, all things change with time. If you stay aware of what is going on in this industry and keep up on whom is making the changes, you will be able to seize opportunities others will miss.

SECTION #12: How Your Behavior Can Affect Your Continued Employment

Recently I was called by a friend in the business, a person that has done many things in the entertainment field and does placement service as well.

She needed 8 Santas to work an event in December that had been done by a select group of fellows for several years. Specific requirements were made from the organizers of this event and I guess over the years their requirements were not met. I had the pleasure of doing this event back in 2012 and 3 of the 8 member team were significantly late and the Santas' conversation was both unhappy and complaining about the situation concerning the hours on site.

This was a 4-hour event that required arrival 1 hour early to avoid having the children seeing any of the Santas before each was placed in his own photo enclosure. The organizers wished to ensure the children would not see more than 1 Santa thus keeping the "secret" alive for these children and their families.

The rate was $100 an hour and we were paid for all 5 hours with a nice free signature meal served after the event was done. The last requirement was that we all wait until the families had cleared the building and we all had changed out of our suits before we could leave.

The "rooms" including the "Green Room" were all inside a large convention center and basically they were framed/curtained off areas keeping each area out of sight from the children. The families were lead to the "room" where their Santa sat waiting for them. Besides 8 Santas this event had 8 photographers and numerous support staff acting as guides and supervisors. Remember the "walls" of the "rooms" were really just fabric.

Well it turns out the organizers of the event sat on the other side of the Green Room walls and could hear all that was said by those inside. They were not eavesdropping; it was simply the way the event was set up. Word I have is that there was some displeasure in 2012 over the Santa "egos" and they had enough after the 2013 event.

So enters a new "Outside HR" placement service that needs 8 Santas for the event in December and she calls me. I gave her the name of a respected and professional Santa that had access to a large Santa database in the So Cal area where this event takes place every year and he has graciously agreed to help my friend find and hire 8 local Professional Santas with liability insurance and background checks and the experience to do this job for the $500 and meal offered. While this is a one day weekend event it takes place in the morning and you are out by 2 pm or so, plenty of time to make late afternoon or evening gigs.

Why am I relating this? Just as in the "Business and Santa Experience" blog written Aug. 6th, 2013, sometimes people will "Sink" their own chances to a position by simply thinking themselves above the "requirements" called for from the "Outsourced HR/Placement service" and they will either miss out on the opportunity to even be in the running like in that "Business and Santa Experience" blog or lose their long held position by ignoring the organizers requirements passed on by a placement service (agent/agency).

It would be very wise to remember the person paying you for your "Professional Services" is your "employer" and should be treated with respect for so long as you are on the job. By fulfilling your obligations/job requirements fully and maintain the Character in character the entire time you are on site, you will likely keep your position working that gig for many years. If you decide to believe your own PR and Hype and place your desires and wishes above and superseding those of your end employer, you will find you have been replaced.

Not just the Santas that were the regulars in that group year after year lost out. The Outsourced HR/Placement Service lost the account as well with their revenue cut due to this account loss. That agency may very well look hard and long before using the "Professionals" that cost them the account. Beyond that, there is communication between the Agents/Agencies that place Santas and they share information. Just as we Santas share trends and information that affects our industry in the form of Santa Schools and blogs.

So I will say to all of you, if you are going to compete and work in the Santa World and this industry, act as if you really enjoy the job and execute and perform to all the requirements set down by the organizers of any event that are passed along by the placement agent to you. To verbally complain on the set anywhere in the hearing of the "Boss" who hired you through the person that is paying you, is a quick ticket to looking for a new position. This also can be exampled with social media. If you work a position and "friend" a set crew on your Facebook account and you complain about something on your page, the "friend" that works the set might just (and often does) pass your problem statement on to higher ups in the company you are working for. The store manager may call and yell at the placement agent and say, "He isn't happy here. Fine! He is out of here and I need a replacement NOW!" It happens more often than you might think.

It is more like "Finding one's place in the world" rather than "The world revolves around ME" especially when you are a Santa.

I have been reading a lot of posts over the last 6 weeks about, for lack of a better term, how the world treats individuals, especially Santas. This is nothing new and will continue to be the case long after I am gone from this scene. In complaining you are giving vent to that which has hurt you and that is normal, even healthy.

However, we as performing Santas have another consideration to make before we dump our laundry for all to see. Remember, if you write it online, it is there for a very long time for anyone to read eventually.

I read recently how one Santa has dedicated his life to charitable acts and in the same thread boasts about buying a restaurant simply to be able to fire a waitress. The thought she was indispensable and though he boasts of his wealth, will complain about the costs of doing business. That is a lot of conflict that need not be reflected by Santa – an individual certainly, but never a Santa.

I have known a Santa performer for over 30 years that seems to truly think the world should revolve around him. Case in point. There are many companies that hire Santa to do performance related venues like malls or other high volume corporate events. My friend is working in a mall this year but for some reason he has not received his drug testing paperwork that must be turned in before he sits in that chair. He feels he should be able to make 1 call and have it resolved. By that I mean he simply makes that call and he expects to be serviced by the home office ASAP. He does not follow up and make calls until he actually speaks to a real person, and then he leaves a message. 1 Santa out of over 400 at the peak of the busy time leading up to the season. To make things even more complicated, there is a time zone involved so when he calls from California in the morning, it is lunchtime there. If he calls in the afternoon around 3pm the office has closed. When asked if he has called about this he says, "I called", then when asked if he spoke to someone about his problem he becomes irate and says, "I left a message!" The problem with this is two-fold. When you sign that 9-page contract YOU have to abide by ALL the stipulations it contains and it is upon the Independent Contractor (You) to make sure they are followed completely. You no do the drug test, you no sit in chair. It is incumbent upon the guy that signs the contract to do everything within his power up to and including making every attempt to contact the employer to fulfill those stipulations.

We are talking about a seasonal job that would pay anywhere from $6000 to $14,000 (he is somewhere in between those values) and he is firmly digging in his feet and has decided to make them call him! Obviously the world revolves around him instead of his seeking where in the world he fits. This is a business and Santas are a commodity that is packaged and marketed to the public. If you are the one doing the marketing booking yourself or you are working for an agency/party planner that sends you out to parties or you work in a mall, you are packaged and presented to the person that hires you to do the job. If you agree to do the job, part of that is to remain in character at all times on set and online.

Yes I said online. Every year, many Santas working for Large Volume Venues do an OUTSTANDING job on set but complained about how they were treated online on Facebook. That seems to be a minor thing but, when you friend someone that works in the shop, you are performing, and they get to read what you write as well. That information is eventually read by the guy that hired you for that position and the next thing you know, you're out the door driving to a different location because the guy that hired you wants nothing to do with you on HIS SET. This is called the "Real World" and that is what happens when a Santa believes he is more important than the customer. They are not interested in why you did not like the child that needed to brush their teeth, the dirty diapers or the child that is ill when placed in your hands. They simply care that you do the job. The public is not worried about those things either as it is their child they have placed in your hands for the picture. The parents are fully aware of the condition of their child. They want the picture, not a lecture.

Just as the customer does not want to hear about how badly you are treated while performing for them, they are not interested in the terrible things you go through to be Santa. They simply want that package they paid for. The one that fits their image of Santa and the appearance you have while sitting in their chair. Anything that keeps you away from that chair when you are scheduled to be in it is a major inconvenience to them and possible breach of the contract you signed. You are the

"Star" of that set and the reason they hire you to be there is to entertain and dazzle the customers that come to have their picture taken with you.

Having too big a self-image will lead to loss of work if your talent is replaceable. One such Santa lost his agent for film work because he told them "I can't come in for audition today, I need at least 3 days to get ready!" The agent dropped him in favor of other Santas that would do what was needed to do the job.

From home visit to top end corporate event, you do the job they hired you for. You sit in the chair they selected. You are dressed for the part and you stay to their script. If you are allowed the freedom of giving your own performance script to the show, it needs to remain within the boundaries of the customer's desire. In other words you need to remain in character at all times as Santa and not talk about politics, the economy, specific religion or the traffic you ran into getting there. None of that is Germane to your performance as it has nothing to do with Santa, only to your interpretation.

In many cases the Rankin-Bass presentation is what the customer is looking for and that is the basis that I start from.

- I simply add to the presentation and keep it in first person.
- I accept any child to visit with me and I stay in character the entire time.
- I submerge my identity and take on that of Santa.

If you are unable to put aside your personal views and take on the simpler world view and mission of Santa you may be in the wrong business.

Santa brings Hope, Joy, Love, Peace, and Acceptance to all that come to him. Yes, I pray but I do not foster my personal religion upon others. The season is stressful enough without me bringing judgment upon the families and children I visit with. Enjoy the Wonders of the Christmas Season and may your Season be Jolly.

SECTION #13: Business And The Santa Experience

This is an example of the "Business of being Santa" that should give you an eye opener.

Recently the Kringle Group owned by Tim Connaghan placed a call for Santas to do a job in Hong Kong. These letters were posted on several boards and groups as an OPEN call.

The Kringle Group
July 30, 2013
I have received a request for a Jolly, real bearded Santa to work in Hong Kong. I thought I had someone for the position, but he has gotten another offer. So the search is on.

This job pays $2,000.00 per week ($6,000.00) and is to work from December 6 to 26. Wednesday would be a day off. Basically 7 hours of work a day: 12:30pm - 3pm, 4:30pm - 6pm, 6:30pm - 8pm.

They will also take care of your airfare, hotel, dry cleaning and meals. Plus they will supply someone to be an interpreter.

If you are interested in this position, please send me information on your experience as Santa. I also need a few photos of yourself and your height, weight and coat size to give to the client.

If you have also worked with any of the mall photo companies, also let me know which ones.

I will be traveling for the next six days, but will be getting my emails and text messages.

Santacerely,
Santa Tim
aka: Santa Hollywood
The Kringle Group
Santa@theKringleGroup.com

Instead of simply sending their information and pictures, many Santas tried to get further information in order to decide if "This" particular position was what they wanted to do.
Then another letter from the Kringle Group had been circulated:

The Kringle Group

August 6, 2013

I thank everyone who applied for the Hong Kong Position. We received over 140 applications and an additional 58 inquiries about this single position in Hong Kong. I only wished there were more positions or openings. You can imagine our surprise that there were so many Santa that were interested in this one job.

If you did not initially send in your photos, experience and measurements when applying, it is now too late to submit. The client is now reviewing only those who sent their information.

In other words, if you did not send the information requested when we sent out the original email, and instead made an inquiry, it is now too late to submit. I apologize for this, but it was the client's decision.

I would suggest in the future for any opportunity, whether with me or any other company, going ahead and sending in your information. In fact, have your resume and a few good photos ready to send. Then when the opportunity appears, you can quickly respond. You can always ask questions later. And if it is not a position you want, or if something is not what you are looking for, you can say no.

I tried to respond to those who asked questions, but unfortunately it was too late in many cases and because we already had the over 140 applications who followed our initial instructions, the client said they have enough good applicants to select from.

In addition, due to the large volume of applications, the client, in China, has narrowed the list by tightening the requirements.

Only those Santas who have real beards, at least 5 years mall experience with a major photo company, have their own wardrobe, and are on the larger size (250 pounds+) are being considered.

Santacerely,
Santa Tim
Santa@theKringleGroup.com

Now this tells us a few things:
First, 140 people did exactly what was asked for and were in the consideration for the job while 58 tried to glean further information and lost out on being part of the "first draft" so to speak. Seems like folks want to see the Orient.

Second, when a call for work such as this goes out, do not think you are the only or best choice! Even if you are, it is a "pig race" where the ones in first might well be the one chosen. Do not waste time asking for more info, if you want the gig, send in your resume and pictures. It is all digital and nearly instantaneous. The 58 that hesitated were out of the running.

Third, the client is now looking at 140 options so feels free to "Narrow" the field with further guidelines/requirements. "Only those Santas who have real beards, at least 5 years mall experience with a major photo company, have their own wardrobe, and are on the larger size (250 pounds+) are being considered. "

While there are 1000s of Santas that fit these requirements, the qualifications say something in themselves: real beards, 5-years' experience in a mall setting, and having their own (suitable) wardrobe and well as having what I refer to as a "Jolly" size (250 + pounds).

I know a little bit more about this from past experience as well. This will be in a hotel (5-star) and your housing and meals will be room serviced (comped) as will all dry cleaning and any in country transportation. Your contract would run for 3 weeks @ $2000 per and you would have a baggage allowance for your flight to allow for extra "carry on" and baggage to cover your Suits as well as your regular luggage. Finally this type of contract includes first class plane fare.

In general you will be treated as an "A" listed celebrity while you're performing. The client is looking for a "Traditional" rendering of the image like a Sundblom or
Nast rendition. SO much for a dieting Santa! Finally the compensation when you include the housing, work schedule, transportation, translator and all the rest, is quite generous compared to many contracts out there with the only "fly" in the mix is the short term of it.

Why am I mentioning these points? Business. The talent pool is going to expand enormously in the next few years as Baby Boomers start to hit retirement age. Instead of 140 applicants you might well see 1400 for the 1 job. What will place you in the consideration is to make your self as competitive and attractive to the potential customer as you can.

Find the work you can do with an eye towards getting experience in the areas that are called for in this ad. Mall settings. This includes sitting in major stares like Macys and Bass Pro Shop and Cabella's to name a few. How do you get these types of work? By educating yourself through schools like the Denver School and IUSC to name two. Then make the connections with those that hire Santa to gain experience. It is a step by step process that will take you time and effort but then you will be able to compete for these jobs.

There is nothing wrong with neither home visits, nor anything wrong with doing charitable events, just as there is nothing wrong with working in a mall or working out of the country. (Make sure your passport is up to date and valid.)

In all respects it is how you decide to approach how to be Santa that will determine what direction you will take in your Santa career. Once you recognize this, you can then decide what school and what direction you wish to go.

When you figure a Santa will have about 60 days tops each year to promote and sell his services, and out of those 60 days might work 40 of them unless locked into a mall contract, you might, maybe garner about 100 hours of experience give or take 30 for the season wearing the Red suit. So factoring in an average of 100 hour experience per year, it would take the average home visit Santa 10 years to accumulate the same amount of experience "in suit" as it would when working a mall for 2 years as your time in the chair working a 49-day contract is between 400 and 500 hours per season working as Santa.

Saying you worked as a professional for 4 years as Santa really does not convey the true story. Sort of like saying you're a professional plumber with all the equipment but for the last 4 years you have only done about 30 to 50 job calls each year. I would want a plumber that goes out on calls 30 to 50 times a month! It is no different with Santa. You gain experience with each year you put under your belt and learn something new every year!

I am NOT running down anyone that has worked as Santa but the truth is, you have limited opportunity to practice your art each year. Schools will help as will going to meetings with groups and clubs. Especially if there are some open and sharing experienced members there that are willing to share their stories. I AM saying that to claim you are PROFESSIONAL and experienced, with only 2-4 seasons under your belt is a little bit shy of the mark you are trying for. It takes about 1000 hours of doing something to become close to being an expert at it. 3 years of mall work will get you to that point with 45+ day contracts. 10 years of home visits will do the same. Even then you will have surprises come from out of left field but by that time you should be able to handle those "Surprises" while maintaining your character and then you have another "funny" story like "the flying baby" experience I had Or the "French kiss by a pit bull" I got working pet night.. I really liked the affection, it was the over tones of liver snacks I could have lived without!

SECTION #14: Experience Matters

Some of you with 5 years under your belt are more than capable to deal with any scenario that may come up while performing as Santa. The clients I refer to in the chapter "Business and Santa Experience" further narrowed the qualifications require to 5 years of Mall experience to even be considered for the position. In this one particular case, the client is requiring that kind of 1000+ hour experience for their employment.

In my dealings with the various party planning placement agents they want a good look for the Santa to send out to represent them. That is a given. Recently when a friend of mine had called several Santas to go and interview for a position (first step in getting the job past having the agent offer you for consideration) she requested all of the Santas in question to make as good a first impression as possible. She gave them a short "check list" to go over prior to showing up for the interview. Little things like clean and neat appearance, groomed hair and beard. Have a jolly demeanor and sharing what experience and beliefs on playing "Santa" they might have in regards to how they interact with children and adults.

One of these gentlemen became exceedingly upset and unhappy with this bit of advice from the person arranging the interview between the Santa and the Client! "How dare she even assume he needed to be told how to interview?

How is it her business to even give advice as she is not a Santa nor never can be? What business was it of hers to even think to offer such advice?"

It is the job of the outsourced HR/Placement agency to make sure you understand the job requirements and the desires/needs of the customer. People go through an agent or agency because they wish to find someone qualified and able to do the job but do not have the time or contacts to find one on their own. This is where the agent/placement service/entertainment agency comes into play. They prescreen and prequalify many possible talents that may be able to perform the job the client want in a suitable fashion. In the case of Mr. "HOW DARE YOU!", he may well be the finest performer around his neck of the woods – in the world perhaps, but the client is not interested in his "ego" and would not care to deal with it on their job. The client may keep the entertainer engaged for the run of the contract but if the actions or words of the performer interfere with the client in any fashion, it will not only reflect poorly on the performer but on the placement agency as well. Thus I fear the example I mentioned may have lost one such "contact" through which he would be employed.

Over the last 33 years I have seen this happen all too often and it is a shame it does. There is nothing wrong with being self-confident, but sometimes in the entertainment industry people write checks with their mouth that their abilities cannot cover. I have seen this with Magicians, Clowns and Santas. The only real cure is experience and the only way to get experience is to perform.

Unfortunately too many people believe they are Equal in ability after 500 hours of training as the person that has 1000 hour or 5000 hours. In every craft I have ever experienced or studied from fishing to target shooting to camping to martial arts to selling retail to model trains to knitting or any other activity, experience and lots of it makes a real and determinable difference.

Any other type of performer has more opportunity to practice their craft all year long gaining experience along the way. While other types of performance will bear on performing the role of Santa, they do not translate directly over, thus the Improv comedian and the clown and the magician and the anachronistic performer – be it pirate, Renaissance Faire player, reenactment performer, musician or storyteller will give additional depth and knowledge to someone playing the part of "Santa". The person that plays the role of Santa exclusively is not going to be as experienced as someone that performs year round playing other roles as well.

The person that plays only Santa is limited to that amount of experience time as compared to someone that has much, much more "time in" playing in character different roles. This often will bear on the choice between two different performers that in all other ways are equal or nearly so. To say it does not, well that is wistful thinking.

That is my point in this book and school and though it would seem to be an unpopular idea, it is true nonetheless. As I have pointed out here, there are ways to increase your total experience time performing and learning the role. Meeting with others that share your interest is a pleasant way to gain knowledge, be it about model trains or being Santa. Looking into other forms of performance that can be done year round is another way to gain experience in front of an audience. Taking up any kind of performance art will be of great help to those that do nothing more than play the role of Santa 2 month out of the year.

Joining internet groups and web pages is yet another means to gain some knowledge but since performance is an interpersonal communication art and many forms of interpersonal communication is lost over the internet such as body language, facial expression and voice inflection and tonal quality, to name a few; this form of learning is limited at best. Much like learning Magic performance strictly from reading a book. Putting theory into practice is far more difficult when there is no example to follow.

In closing, you can agree or not, it matters not to me as I do not charge for advice. What I pass on is simply the fruit of my 33+ years of performance experience. Not everyone has had the same experiences or results as I have and I admit there is much I still learn from others. But do not mistake the truth that experience matters. In all activities, the more experience you have, the better your performance of that activity will be.

SECTION #15: What Can A Santa Do The Rest Of The Year?

This applies to everyone but I started this talk back in 2004 as part of the presentation I gave at Tim's IUSC and at the 2006 Branson convention. This was originally for RBS but the information is applicable to Mrs. Claus and Traditional Bearded Santas as well.

So you have invested a great deal of time and money into your Santa presentation. That is Great! But you sit there with nothing to do for 10 months out of the year, as there is very little for a Santa to do outside of the Christmas season.

Oh sure, there is the odd "Christmas in July" events and you might get into doing advertising work with video or film but those are rather few and far between. So, what to do?

You can take the experience you gained from learning the role of Santa and apply it to other "Characters". You have learned how to research a character to gain both background and depth for the personality you are trying to play. You have also learned where and how to put together an authentic looking period costume. Now you can use that knowledge to develop new characters you can perform the rest of the year. This Blog will help you do just that with character and venue suggestions.

We will start with the selection process and proceed from there. Do you have a favorite character from history or fiction? Perhaps you are a Civil War historian or you really like stories centered on the Old West. You could like going to the Renaissance Faire or like the writings of Shakespeare. Perhaps the Colonial period or the French Revolution is what you like to read about. Perhaps you simply wish to relive the 60's.

Here is a partial list of character suggestions that might start your imagination:

- **Renaissance Faire:** Brewer-Blacksmith-Scholar-Noble-Baker-Butcher-Printer-Apothecary-Sell Sword-Mendicant-Wizard...
- **Old West:** Western Judge aka "Roy Bean"-Barkeep-Gold Panner-Trail Cook-Miner 49'r-Mule Skinner-Fur Trapper-Mountain Man-Pony Express Rider-Marshall-Sheriff-Johnny Appleseed-Pecos Bill-Buffalo Hunter...
- **Civil War:** General from either side-Steamboat Captain-Artillery Officer-Naval Officer-Ship Wright-Wagon Master-Ranking Politician from either side-Dry Goods shop owner-Cattle Herder-Lumber Jack-Army Surgeon...
- **Victorian/Dickens:** Professor-Banker-Judge-Doctor-Trades Man-Train Magnate-Magistrate-any character from the Dickens Novels such as Scrooge or any character from Jules Verne's writings...
- **Sailing:** Pirate Captain-First Mate- Whaling Ship-Clipper Ship-Harpooner-Any Sailor from before the Mast-Robinson Crusoe-Treasure Island-The Voyages of the Beagle-Sir Francis Drake...

- **Historical War Periods:** The Revolutionary War-The War of 1812-The Cuban Revolution-The Spanish/American War...
- **Others:** Old Hippy-Hill Billy-Biker-Neptune-Zeus-Poseidon-ZZ Top-Barbarian (What's in your wallet?)-Caveman...

Now that you have picked out the character you want to play you have much the same work you invested into being Santa before you can play the new character.

Now you must research the character history and try to be contemporary to the time period he lived in. This means learning the speech patterns and idioms of the time he lived or is placed in (if fictional). Remember this is a "living history" portrayal of someone that lived in the past.

You would not recognize a cell phone or tablet as such and would try to fit it into your "then" world view. Most important is to stay in first person while presenting and acting your new character.

Learn the important events of the timeline he came from. Learn the customs and slang of the period as well as the mannerisms. In other words, try to do the same job as you did with Santa to make this a believable presentation.

Next you will need to build an outfit with props that will fit in as many ways as possible to the time period you are supposed to have come from. From the top of your head down to your feet this needs to be addressed. Avoid the use of plastic and synthetics as much as possible. From the 1820's on, there was limited mass production in the way of clothing but still attention to detail is a must.

Now you have selected your character and you have done your homework in developing a timeline, background story and outfitted yourself in a convincing period costume. Now it is time to find work and venues to perform!

You had to find ways to promote your Santa portrayal and many of the venues and agencies you now work with will be interested in your new character.

Another role for Santa to play

Entertainment agencies, Gig Salad, networking through clubs and gatherings, The Rotary Club meetings, Chamber of Commerce meetings will all give you exposure and help you find shows to perform.

Watch for events. If your new persona is related to an upcoming movie at the theater, contact the theater to see if they want you there in character where while working for tickets and popcorn you hand out your card to patrons while posing for pictures. Have picture business cards and flyers made promoting your new act/character. Be sure to have them handy when you go out in character.

Restaurants will hire themed performers for children's night. Chick-fil-A will have Pirate night or Old West night or Star Wars night. They even have Fairy Princess Night complete with horse drawn princess carriage.

Schools will have learning modules on various periods in history: the Revolutionary War, The War of Succession, The Renaissance, The Gold Rush and The Old West. They will hire educational shows for assemblies. You basically give a monolog about the life and times you are playing for 30 to 45 minutes answering questions.

Other sources for contacts and employment would be Street Fairs, Farmers Markets, Costume shops, Magic shops, Costume Rental shops, Party stores and City or Regional Parks & Recreation Depts.

I have been doing this since 1981 and it helps to have multiple characters to present. Before each performance I review my notes on the character I am to play. I go over the time line and refresh my memory on the main important characters or people that are involved with the world my character came from. Just like remembering the names of the reindeer.

I hope your enjoy your new adventures in entertainment!

SECTION #16: Insurance Sources

Once upon a time, way back in 2008, you could only get Santa Insurance from one source, FORBS. Too be sure you could get entertainers insurance but at a much higher cost. That one source was one of the main reasons people joined that group. Not because they particularly like the group but because they could get the insurance relatively inexpensively.

Flash forward to 2013 and you can now get Santa insurance from a number of locations. I am going to mention several in this section. Most of the selections are various shades of vanilla but there is one major stand out and that is why I list that group first. All of the examples require you pass a background check that generally costs around $19.95 and you do have to be a member of the group you are buying insurance through. Prices stated as of 2013:

1. **Nationwide Santas** www.NationwideSantas.com
   $210.00 - $3 million in liability with $500,000 abuse/molestation rider with current background check. For an additional $50 fee, you can be covered for any act you perform with some restrictions.
2. **Clowns of Canada** www.clownscanada.com
   $150 - $2 million policy and $250 for $5 million coverage.

For an additional fee you can insure your equipment through this company. HUB International, 3063 Walker Rd. Windsor, ONT. N8W 3R4

3. **IBRBS International Brotherhood of Real Bearded Santas** www.ibrbsantas.org $185 - $2 million and $210 for the $4 million coverage with $300,000 abuse/molestation rider with current background check.

4. **FORBS Fraternal Order of Real Bearded Santas** www.FORBSsantas.com
$185 - $2 million and $210 for the $4 million coverage with $300,000 abuse/molestation rider with current background check

5. **SOS Society of Santa** www.SocietyofSanta.org $145 + $30 (application fee) for a total of $175 for the $2 million liability coverage. $300,000 molestation rider when you pass the FBI background check. Insurance does cover you for other than "Santa" performances. Membership in SOS does require proof of insurance of this type. SOS has no dues but they do charge a $30 "application fee" and you have a background check cost as well.

6. **LSS-Lone Star Santas** http://lonestarsantas.org $210 plus membership and background check for $4 million total amount $2 million coverage per occurrence. Must be a member of LSS and have a background check. Membership in LSS requires a background check.

7. **Specialty Insurance Agency US and Canada** coverage. www.specialtyinsuranceagency.com $215 per person - No dues or fees. This is group coverage and that means the $5 million pool of coverage shrinks with each claim from any of the hundreds of Santas covered under it.

Must be a WCA member, dues are $40 a year $2 million policy $139.00 a year with a $30 fee for each COI naming additional insured's

8. **K&K Insurance** www.kandkinsurance.com/Pages/Home.aspx
9. **WCA** / World Clown Association: www.worldclown.com
10. $200 per person – No dues or fees.
    Entertainer's insurance with a $5 million limit individual coverage for incomes under $30,000 a year.

There are many more groups and clubs that have insurance available to their membership. Just about all require the background check and you will only be covered for your Santa performances. With a few exceptions, such as WCA, K&K and Nationwide Santas, you can get additional insurance for year-round performances.

While having some insurance is a good thing, certain venues require a minimum level. For instance, Bass Pro Shop requires a $2 million coverage policy, so you have to buy the $2 million or better policy most groups offer to be able to work at such a venue. Prices do move up or down (rarely) each year so this information on pricing may not be accurate next year. You can find more information on carriers and issuers of insurance on the "Santa and the Business of being Santa" Facebook group.

SECTION #17: Ethics – What Are They And How They Apply To The Santa World

Google "Ethics" and you will find About 49,800,000 results (0.32 seconds). There are Business Ethics, Personal Ethics, Situational Ethics, Work Ethics and many more such topics.

On a practical level ethics are very different from person to person. That means the ethics of the person you are dealing with may not be the same as yours or meet the level of acceptance in the community they are working in. Ethics can be moral but Morals are not Ethics.

"Like Baumhart's first respondent, many people tend to equate ethics with their feelings. But being ethical is clearly not a matter of following one's feelings. A person following his or her feelings may recoil from doing what is right. In fact, feelings frequently deviate from what is ethical.

"Nor should one identify ethics with religion. Most religions, of course, advocate high ethical standards. Yet if ethics were confined to religion, then ethics would apply only to religious people. But ethics applies as much to the behavior of the atheist as to that of the devout religious person. Religion can set high ethical standards and can provide intense motivations for ethical behavior. Ethics, however, cannot be confined to

religion nor is it the same as religion." (Santa Clara University/Markkula Center for applied Ethics)

This is not going to cover all the facets of ethics but it will look at how poor ethics and situational ethics have affected this business of being Santa.

Let's look at some of the things that have happened in the not so distant past.

There is an incident with an individual that managed to sell the idea of a convention to a hotel chain, a convention center, a township and a MLB team with each of them signing contracts with this person under his promise to deliver 300 attendees to the event and very possibly more. Just 2 years before, a groundbreaking event similar in nature had taken place in Branson and this Branson experience was a big success! What the new promoter failed to show to these organizations was the rapid loss in his membership and he also failed to give an honest detailing of his experience in this field. In essence, "his" truths were not totally and completely kept. The Hotel, MLB team and Convention center all provided incentive payments and perks to have this individual sign contract agreements to hold said event with them. (http://marathonpundit.blogspot.com/2007/07/kansas-blogging-santa-convention-coming.html & http://aorbsinc.com/newsletters/jinglevolliss]pdf.

Over the course of the next 10 months, this individual fired or replaced all the help he had in organizing this event and he tried to do it himself, with predictable results. **He failed**. Yet those contracts were signed and unfortunately there was nothing the holders of the contacts could go after since the person responsible had no assets other than his rapidly shrinking club. The people of Overland Park ended up losing jobs, money and because money was spent in preparation of this "Major Convention", the losses could not be recovered. Something like 12 Santas were at the Ball Game to have their picture taken but the seats that would have been sold to all the promised attendees were empty as were the rooms held for the attendees to stay and the convention center for the event to be held in.

Was he ethical in not giving truthful numbers and an accounting of his abilities and experience in this field of organization? On the bright side of things, the several cases of Cracker Jacks that were altered and resealed did end up at yet another poorly planned and executed event a few years later at the first Celebrate Santa event run by Joe Moore. Somewhat like passing the torch in failed or tainted events it turned out.

There have been other large-scale events tried under the same set of conditions. Whenever done by people of "flexible" ethics, it has not gone well for those that were partners with the operator. It seems that a LOT of people lost money and time in these events except for the person that organized them unethically.

On a smaller scale entertainers of all types have issues with their ethics that come back on them in various degrees of difficulty to them. You offer a service to the public as an "Independent Contractor" entertainer. Once you have agreed to do a service for a customer and have agreed to a price and or accepted a deposit or retainer, YOU have entered into a contract with that customer. This can have consequences if you do not fulfill your end of the contract.

At one extreme is a case from the UK recently.

"A Northern Ireland DJ who cancelled bookings on the morning of weddings by falsely claiming his father had died has been convicted of theft. The Trading Standards Authorities (TSA) said in a statement that he "promised to deliver a service and failed to do this".

"His excuse for cancelling on four different occasions between the start of August 2012 and end of September that year was that his father had died the previous day or morning," the TSA said." (http:// www.bbc.co.uk/news/uk-northern-ireland-25987165)

While this case was taken to court and tried with a conviction, the method is common in practice here in the US by unethical entertainers. All types of home entertainment Independent Contractors have these types of people that give their entire business a bad name.

Incidents like this: the Clown that has "wrecked her vehicle" 5 times over the course of a month; the Magician that had to cancel his show "because of a death in the family" so many times it was a wonder there were any left to come to the family reunion; and the Santa that backs out of the Bookings because he is retiring from the business only to go behind the booking agent to contact the client directly.

These types of entertainers are a problem for all the rest of us in that they "Poison the Well" of the customer base for any future performer. Not only are the customers disenchanted and disinterested in booking a performer, when they do it is an uphill climb for the next performer to overcome the bad experience and satisfy the customer expecting the worst before you even show up.

In each of the above examples, Greed was a motivating factor.

In the case of the Clown and Magician, they simply would over book themselves and then take the highest paying show. Sometimes the performer would then try to get the lesser paying shows covered but would not overly stress the point if he or she could not and simply "destroy" another vehicle or "kill" off another relative. Often times the same one in both cases.

In the case of the Santa, beyond Greed there is also an innate Laziness factored in. The Santa had waited for the agency to line up the customers and book the shows having secured the Santa to do them. Then all the Santa had to do is "Quit the Business" separating himself from the agency and then go directly to the customer and offer a direct service deal at a lower price than the agency but a much higher price than what he had agreed to at the time of the booking. I am sure the Santa in question thought it was a WIN/win situation all around. By cutting out the middleman (agency) and going direct, the customer saves money and he makes more! Small problem with this as in the larger examples, agents in the business talk to each other. Yes, if you are smart enough and clever enough to do this on the QT and manage to get enough of the customers to go with you, you could make as much as 25% to 40% more than you would have if you had stood on your word and honored the deal you made with the agency, but only if you are very good and somewhat lucky. In the case of conventions and large-scale events, there are back channel communications that happen between the convention businesses and between Hotels. They even have regularly published trade papers and magazines that report this sort of thing.

However the next year, do you really expect any agency that also communicates with the one you wronged to pick you up for any real amount of work? You can pretty much forget working for that last agency as well.

Who would take a chance on employing you to do a job for them if they know you are likely to steal the job by offering your services direct? Going to start up your own agency? I wish you the best of luck in that. If you thought being Santa was expensive, wait till you get a look at the advertising costs! They are a 12 month commitment!

How can this be dealt with and or avoided? We as individuals can look a little harder at the people that are putting on the event and look at their history of what they have accomplished. Then Folks can start asking questions as to where your money is going and how much the difference is between paying for your own meals and the price that is set for the event. A $15-$18 meal at the restaurant charged out at $30-$45 is telling you there is nice profit going somewhere. Check around to see what rooms actually cost away from the "host" hotel. Getting a rate of $100 a night is great compared to the $200 the hotel "normally" charges but before you plunk down you money, call and see what kind of discounts you can have through various options on your own or through a travel agency. Then look at the hotels and motels in the general area for price comparison. Spend your money wisely and get the best value you can.

In the case of individuals doing such unethical practices, there really isn't much we can do except bring these practices to light and make sure we are all aware of who is damaging our community reputation. If the performer continues after having his or her actions exposed, the lack of support from the community will slow and discourage that person. Eventually they will either clean up their act or they will move on to other forms of business as the opportunities and money dries up.

In Magic it is the magician that does not have the talent, equipment or experience to pull off the job he low bid on.

In Clowning it is the "First of May" that bid the job for less than the materials cost hoping to break into the business without the experience or equipment to do the job they bid on.

In the Santa World it is the Santa that bids low and simply overbooks with an eye towards taking the highest paying gig and not really caring what happens to the families he does not manage to visit.

Wanting to "break into" the business is something we all face and deal with when starting out. Like many things in life, it is HOW we go about this that frames our reputation in the community we serve and the community we compete in.

Cell Phone is DEDUCTABLE inc. PLAN
Santa School "   "

SECTION #18: Taxes And You The Santa

That time of year is coming again but you should have been working on this year round. I do a long form every year now for over 29 years simply because doing the short form with 1099s will lead to paying taxes that you cannot use your deductions to offset. The very first time I ran across the "self-employment tax" which is basically the social security portion your employer pays through your W-2, you could hear my yell across 2 counties! Then the Tax professional and I sat down and talked about the things I could deduct legally from my taxes and what I had to keep records of.

I am not a Tax professional and I do recommend that you seek out the advice of a good Tax accountant if you are going to be an entertainer/Santa and take payment for your work. It will save you money over the long run and help you avoid difficulties with the IRS.

I will give you examples of some of the things I have been advised to take as deductions against my tax liability over the years and then I will also add an internet report with a link to it from such a tax expert as well.

Itemized deductions I have taken on my taxes:

- SANTA SUIT. Each time I purchase a new Santa suit I have been able to deduct the cost of it from my taxes as it is part of my business.

Along with that, all of the accessories I have bought to go with those suits such as Boots, Belts and small items like bags and bells. Also the repair and cleaning of these items are tax deductible.
- CELL PHONE. My cell phone is a deduction, not just the cost of the phone itself but the cell service as well. I conduct business and use my phone to stay in touch via the internet with email and social media with business contacts. I would not be able to conduct my business at the level I currently do without this device and those services.
- MILEAGE. The mileage I drive to and from a job/gig is deductible.
- SUPPLIES. Any and all expendable such as giveaways, candy canes and the like are a deduction.
- ADVERTISING. All manner of media used to advertise my business including web sites, business cards, flyers, or any other means of advertising is a deduction.

EDUCATIONAL MATERIALS. Related to your profession such as books, periodicals, DVDs, computer software, as well as Schools, attending Professional meetings and conventions are a business expense and therefor a deduction. This includes travel to and from such events, per Diem meals and housing expense, and any other expense incurred involving your interaction with other professionals during said event.

TRANSPORTATION. In other transportation costs, if you need to hire a taxi or rent a vehicle or any other form of transportation related to the completion of a job or job related event that too is a deduction.

COMPUTER. If you use your computer to conduct business your internet connection is deductible in some cases as is the purchase of new equipment or repair to older units used in your business. This includes upgrade to your software.

Basically if you buy something to be used in your performance or to conduct your business, it is a business expense and can be deducted. Keep in mind you might not want to use all of your deductions every year as you must show a profit more often than loss or the IRS could disallow your activities as a business and classify it as a hobby and therefore not deductible.

Here is the article online.

http://www.howtodothings.com/finance-and-money/a2779-how-to-take-tax-deductions-for-actors-and-entertainers.html

How To Take Tax Deductions for Actors and Entertainers
By M. E. Hill

Actors, singers, dancers, and other performers face some challenges when trying to prepare their tax returns. While this article covers the essentials of filing a correct return, you can only benefit from treating your work as a business and taking some classes in business law - busy performers can now take these courses online.

In any case, irregular payments, unusual business-related expenses, and supplemental income in the form of "regular" jobs all add up to a more complicated than average tax return.

Many artists end up with a combination of income types: income from regular wages and income from self-employment. Income from wages involves a regular paycheck with all appropriate taxes, social security, and

Medicare withheld. Income from self-employment may be in the form of cash, check, or goods, with no withholding of any kind.

The business-related expenses are deducted differently for each type of income, and you will need to complete several different forms in order to do so.

Review the guidelines below to determine the correct way to deduct your expenses.

If you get a regular paycheck: If you've got a gig lasting more than a few weeks, chances are you will get paid regular wages with all taxes withheld. At the end of the year, your employer will issue you a form W-2. If this regular paycheck is for entertainment-related work (and not just for waiting tables to keep the rent paid), you will deduct related expenses on a Schedule A, under "Unreimbursed Employee business expenses," or on Form 2106, which will give you a total to carry to the schedule A.
The type of expenses that go here are:

- Union dues.
- Apparel: Uniforms, costumes, special shoes (tap, ballet, character, or anything else not suitable for street wear) theatrical makeup, and wigs.
- Cleaning of work-related apparel.
- Education: Acting, voice, or dance lessons, or other education related to improving or maintaining your performance skills.
- Photographs, videos, or CDs used for self-promotion and marketing.

If you are considered an independent contractor: Independent contractors get paid by cash or check with no withholding of any kind. This means that you are responsible for all of the Social Security and Medicare normally paid or withheld by your employer; this is called Self-Employment Tax. In order to take your deductions, you will need to complete a Schedule C, which breaks down expenses into even more detail. In addition to the items listed above, you will probably have items in the following categories: Advertising: Promotional and marketing materials go here, as do any ads you place offering your services.

- Legal and professional fees: Commissions to agents, attorney fees, and tax preparation fees go here. You can also put union dues here if the membership is not tied to any one job.
- Auto/transportation expenses: Track your mileage to auditions, keep receipts for the bus or subway, and hang on to plane and train ticket info.
- Insurance: Any special insurance or bond required because of your work. NOTE: Health insurance is deducted elsewhere, so don't include that here.
- Supplies: Shoes, costumes, makeup and office supplies go here.
- Other: Postage, cell phone if devoted exclusively to work, fax or photocopy fees, classes, reference materials, subscriptions, and anything else related to getting or performing work. If in doubt, keep

the receipt, note what it was for, and ask your tax professional or the IRS.

If you have a combination of income types: You will be better off subtracting as many expenses as you can on the Schedule C, since this will lower your Self Employment Tax. If an expense relates to both types, either put it all on the C or break it down and put a percentage on the C. Don't lie, but take the time to figure out what can legitimately be deducted against each type of income.

If all of this seems overwhelming or confusing: Go to a professional tax preparer. The most important thing for you to do is keep track of your income and expenses; you can always pay someone to put everything in the right place on the right form for you. But good recordkeeping is crucial. Even the best tax professionals cannot save you money or keep you out of trouble if you don't have good records. Keep all receipts, even if you just throw them in a big envelope marked "Taxes." Note daily expenses in whatever kind of calendar you use for appointments. The IRS loves to see stuff in writing. And don't forget the benefit of educating yourself; taking even a few online classes in business tax law can help you keep your company (yourself) from being faced with problematic tax issues.

Quick Tips:
When adding up your expenses, keep all similar expenses together. Put all shoes, costumes and makeup under "Apparel" and so on.

Remember that if you are self-employed and pay for your own health insurance, you can deduct that on page 1 of your 1040.

Navigate to the IRS.GOV website and search for these useful forms and instructions:
IRS Schedule C
IRS Schedule C Instructions
IRS Form 2106
IRS Form 2106 Instructions

SECTION #19: "The Checklist"

Many people have a tendency to put off something until the last minute and then they are stressed trying to "get it done" in time. Don't believe me? Look at the lines for tax preparation or how folks get in a rush right after Thanksgiving. Those that work in the Santa industry are much the same. That is why this blog it titled "The Checklist".

This list of things "to do" will help you keep your business on track and minimize stress along the way to a successful Christmas season.

October

Flu season is going to start soon so get in to talk to your doctor now. By getting the flu shot now you will be fully protected before the flu season starts. Make time to talk to your doctor and discuss what is coming up. Make sure he/she understands you will be coming into contact with 100's or even 1000's of children and need to take steps to keep healthy.

Beyond the basic flu shot, you might want to get the pneumonia vaccination as well and while you have the doctor's attention, discuss ways to boost your immunity and staying healthy. Now is also a good time to go over any prescriptions you may have and make sure you have enough to carry you through the Christmas season.

Follow your doctor's advice.

Schedule a dental appointment and cleaning.

Make an appointment with your local mechanic to check over your vehicle as well. Brakes, tires, get the anti-freeze checked. Talk to the mechanic about what you will be doing during the winter and all the driving you will be doing. Follow his/hers advice because a breakdown during season will make it difficult for you to keep your appointed rounds. If you live in an area where it snows, check your chains to be sure they will fit the tires you have on your vehicle and are in good repair. Also check your spare tire and inventory the tools that are supposed to be in your car. Nothing worse than having a flat and your jack is missing.

November

First week

Now is the right time to do your Christmas shopping. Write, stamp and seal those Christmas cards and set them aside until closer to black Friday, ready to go.

Take out your suit from storage and take it over to your dry cleaner to have it gone over. Make sure all the stitching is tight, that the suit is fresh and clean and get it scotch guarded before the end of the first week of November. Then hang it up ready to go.

Buy the staples you will need and stock your pantry. Do this before Thanksgiving Day to avoid the rush. Don't forget the "comfort" foods.

Second week

Fill your prescriptions, and get some cough drops just in case.

Make sure you schedule some down time for yourself during the coming season to spend with your friends and family. Have a large format calendar up on the wall with your appointments listed on each date between now and New Year's Day. Also have that information listed in your appointment book and make sure to check both to make sure they both say the same thing.

Third week

Get your vehicle checked once more and get your oil changed and your car serviced.

Mail your cards and letters. Send out those packages and gifts.

Polish your boots and metal work. Check the rest of your equipment and props.

Make sure you pay up your cell phone bill.

Make sure you keep up your exercise routine and eat a balanced diet.

Things to keep in the car: have your "kit" ready in the car. In this kit you should have items that will make your visits easier.

- White hair color for touch ups as needed. I use Ben Nye white mascara for this.
- breath mints.
- Comb and brush.
- small flash light
- deodorant
- snacks like dried fruit, nuts, granola
- water
- mouthwash and toothbrush
- small scissors and mirror
- safety pins of various sizes
- small sewing kit
- cough drops
- small first aid kit and aspirin
- list of the day's appointments with directions and contact numbers on a clip board
- cell phone charger for auto
- extra pairs of white gloves
- shoe polish
- a role of black electricians tape
- Some loose change like quarters for vending machines

A mall kit might also include:

- Febreeze

- a supply of any meds you may need for a week
- a few hand rags or paper towels
- extra glasses
- a phone wall charger
- waterless hand cleanse
- hairspray
- spray disinfectant
- tissue
- a few small light up toys and/or stuffed animals
- be sure to have a light meal or two for each day in the mall that is easy to fix but nonperishable
- Hair care tools
- a book and deck of cards

Daily check list during season:

- Walk around the vehicle and look at the tires.
- Make sure you have fuel. Don't let your tank get under half full during season if you can help it.
- Have "weather gear" like a rain suit that fits and an umbrella in the car.
- Keep a bootjack in the car in case you need to take your boots off while out on the road.
- Keep a set of footwear and clothing in the car.
- Eat a balanced diet and get your rest.

A side note about working the mall, I have found it helpful to have a supply of chocolate handy to toss to the "helpers" while on break. It is a stress reliever for them and they in turn are far more inclined to be helpful to Santa in return. I also have been known to bring in fresh fruit to the break room that any and all can partake from. Let's face it, this is not a high paying job and most of these folks are doing this to make a little money for Christmas presents. Staying jolly is only half the battle; keeping your crew in good spirits is very important in making the experience a good one for the visitors that come to see Santa.

A few "Don't s"

Don't speed. Make sure you have plenty of time between appointments to get from one to the next. You want to arrive intact, relaxed and without a speeding ticket.
Don't skip meals.

- Don't forget to take your medicine.
- Don't use your cell phone while driving. Get a "hands free" blue tooth device if you must talk while driving.
- Don't take your phone onto the set
- Don't frown while driving. Remember you're visible to all the other drivers and their little passengers.
- Don't forget to have fun.

SECTION #20: Magic And Santa

My name is Gordon Bailey and I have been a magic hobbyist for over 44 years and a performer for over 30 of those years. While one does not preclude the other, being a hobbyist first has added depth and experience to my performance. I went into performing as a way to make a living due to injury and no longer being able to perform my work in the lumber mill. During my years of performance I have done shows in South Korea, a layover in Osaka on the way home, in a plane over the middle of the pacific headed home, farmers markets performing in the round, on stage, in the street, in auditoriums, in class rooms, in outdoor events and parks, in hospitals, in back yards and in living rooms from California to Florida. I perform magic shows, develop magic routines and teach the art of magic to others.

From the beginning of my Santa performing I have worked to incorporate magic into the presentation of Santa thereby enhancing the idea that Santa is magical. Many of the things Santa does in the routine of his job are explained away by magic that only he can perform. By performing small effects up close with the children while visiting you re-enforce that idea in the mind of the child making your performance much more "Real".

There are many "Christmas Magic" effects available on the market and there are as many other "utility" props that can be worked into a Christmas theme by developing the proper "patter". Such items as the "Clippo Candy Cane", the "6 foot tall appearing Candy Cane", and the foam "Lump of coal to present" are examples of just a few items available commercially. One I developed specifically to meet a need with the "Polar Express" story was to go to Krissi Peters and design a "mini Santa Sack change bag" expressly for the purpose of forcing ringing or non-ringing bells like those in the story. Here is an example of how I used the Santa Sack change bag.

The role of a wizard is another character for Santa to play in the off season.

In 2002 I did a Girl Scout slumber Christmas Party that one of the Mrs. Claus (Robyn Marquardt) had booked and wanted me to go with her to read the "Polar Express". When Robyn and I arrived at the home of the party, there were some 30 young ladies aged 6-8 and one little boy about 5.

Mrs. Claus had taken the time to wrap a gross of bells individually in tissue and had me give out the bells, 1 each to every child. During this time the little boy kept dancing around with a frown on his face shouting "You're Not Santa, You're Not Santa!" until one of the parents caught him and quieted him down.

I then instructed the children not to open their "gift" until Mrs. Claus told them to. I then proceeded to read the story and of course the point of it is, as long as you believe, you will hear the bells. Well the story ended and the children opened their gift to find the bell and they all started ringing them! It was quite a clamorous noise. The parents were happy, the girls were happy and Mrs. Claus was happy. But just then I felt a tug on my sleeve and as I looked down the little boy had tears in his eyes and said "Santa, My bell doesn't ring!"

Mrs. Claus was right beside me and was shocked as well. How that one child managed to get the only bell that did not ring was totally beyond me! What are the odds? As I bent over to take his bell to "inspect" I was holding my left hand behind me and Mrs. Claus put another bell in it. I then did a "Mulholland" switch substituting the non-ringer for the new and said, "Try it now". Of course the bell rang and that boy became a believer!

I then spent the rest of that year and part of the following January trying to come up with a way to do that on command that fit into the Santa theme. The "Santa's Magic Bag" was the fruit of that experience – a change bag that looks like a Santa Bag, only in miniature.

Krissi Peters of Harlequin Costume makes them still and they are of the highest quality. Of course there are alternatives, but to my research and knowledge there was no "Santa's Magic Bag" before Krissi made the first one for me.

I still have the original prototype and recently purchased a new one from her vendor table at the reunion luncheon. The original lasted 9 years before it finally wore out. Krissi makes the finest example I have yet to see but there are similar bags made all over now or you could try to order a red "ickle pickle" change bag for the same purpose. Krissi's just looks more the part because of the attention to detail and the materials match the suit. Other effects simply lend themselves to a Christmas theme even if they were not designed for such originally. "Gold and Silver" is one such effect. With a few minor props, "Gold and Silver" can be used to illustrate the story of St Nicholas and the three sisters. I worked up the patter and shared it with Santa Sam Sidoti who went on to use it with great success.

A "peek" mentalism wallet will keep your business card in the wallet of a potential customer for years. A thumb tip that lights up is very popular these days. Having a "squeaker" makes dolls "talk" that never made a sound before. Having had learned how to "palm" a coin is a valuable skill. There are many magic items that can be adapted to a Christmas theme and the only true limitation is your imagination.

In this section of the School, I will demonstrate the usage of such props and effects to enhance the Santa performance along with examples of patter and sources of where to find such items. Using these props and or attending my school would not make you a magician but it would start you on a path to a better, stronger, more entertaining performance as Santa. The use of magical effects properly applied will illustrate the story you are telling about Santa and why his world is magical. The most important idea I would be trying to import to the folks that attend the school would be the prop is secondary to the presentation. Your patter and ease of presentation would be far more important than the effect itself. This will only come with practice and if you "own" the trick by practicing it until the moves and patter are automatic; then, the simplest effect becomes magical in the eyes of the audience.

Here are some Magic References: Try to forgo the Internet and instead go into a real magic store if you can. The help and instruction you will receive from the shop owner after your purchase is very valuable! If on the other hand you simply must go through internet sources for your magic purchase, here are some suggestions to choose over the many out there:

- For reading I suggest the Klutz Book or Magic which is a wonderful beginner volume full of professional close up magic written in easy to understand terms with the props included.
- A bit more advanced study would be the Tarbell Course in Magic with 8 volumes of study. It truly is the encyclopedia of Magic.
- I really like the Magic Makers series of DVD video lessons on the different forms of magic.
- The 4 DVD set of Modern Coin Magic will give you the palming skills you will find useful.
- 30 Tricks & Tips with Magic Sponge balls is also a really good lesson set

Master those and get a book or 8 and you are well on your way to gaining the skills of Magic.

It is my hope that if you attend the "Santa and the Business of being Santa school, you will come away with several ideas use. Everything we have in life is on loan, even the food we eat. Feel free to take the ideas I will be presenting and make them your own.

SECTION #21: Profitable Activities For Mrs. Claus And Elves

What does an Elf or Mrs. Claus do at an event? Not just a home visit or small party but a full blown corporate event or mall? This workshop will address all of these venues in depth utilizing much of the experience garnered over the last 30 years of organizing Christmas event crews. We will start with the home visit and work our way up to the corporate event.

First of all, the reason Mrs. Claus and/or Elves would be there is for profit enhancement. In other words, the customer wants to have entertainment and diversions provided for their guests beyond having Santa sit in a chair to have pictures taken, stories told and presents given out and they want it provided in theme. That is where the Elves and Mrs. Claus come in. At a strictly photo session engagement, to complete the set the photographer could be an Elf or Mrs. Claus. That is to say the person taking the pictures is a professional photographer dressing and acting the part because the pictures are a high priority to the customer. Additional Elves are of use in line management and assisting the child to and from Santa. In this case the character involved is secondary to the function being performed but they add to the ambiance of the set just as the chair and backdrop. That is the minimal engagement of characters but there is much more that can be done!

With a party setting and home visit there are many things Mrs. Claus or an Elf can do in this venue. Storytelling, candy cane distribution, posing for pictures, gift distribution, song leading as well as profit enhancing activities such as:

- Cookie Decorating: Use store bought, preferably individually wrapped sugar cookies for this event for protection from litigation. I know that there are some fantastic cookie makers out there but the manufacturers have much deeper pockets in the event of some misadventure resulting from the cookies. It is NOT the cookie that is the focus of this activity but the child's interaction while decorating it. Along with the cookies you will need assorted tubes of frosting in various colors; sprinkles in tubes also in various colors, wrapped candies and a drop cloth of some kind would also be advisable. It would also be nice to provide small aprons for the children to wear while they "work" in the "Cookie Factory". Have the sprinkles, frosting tubes and candies arranged on a worktable and give each child 1 cookie to work with at a time. This will keep the children happily occupied for many minutes and parents will be happy taking pictures of their "Master Cookie Chef" at work. All items used and opened are for use at that one event and not to be carried over to the next for customer safety.

- Make your own Christmas Card: For this you will need brightly colored construction paper half sheets, glue sticks, foam decorations in seasonal shapes. Crayon markers and pens, spray glitter and craft glitter, perhaps a few sheets of stick on gems. Also a drop cloth and the aprons will be very handy in keeping things neat and clean. Here the position is mainly supervisory keeping the supplies on the table and making sure they are shared among all that come. You can also have a "Make your own ornament" table using wooden blanks in the shape of stars or fir trees along with the same materials used in card making.

- Mrs. Claus "Cooking Demonstration": This is really just taking a small mason jar and all the ingredients for making hot cocoa. You demonstrate "Santa's" favorite cocoa recipe by putting the ingredients into the mason jar one layer at a time. Powdered milk, cocoa, sugar or equal, cinnamon to taste, marshmallows (mini of course) filling the jar and then add the lid and decorate with ribbons and bows. Makes a wonderful gift of the season with a personal touch and the layers of color from the various ingredients is fun to arrange. To prepare, all they have to do is add the contents of the jar to very hot water and stir. Many things can be added to this formula such as flavor crystals, nutmeg and or some coffee powder along with chocolate chips. Whatever your tastes run to, just remember that a little nutmeg goes a long way. Once your demonstration is done, you invite the audience to make their own "secret recipe" to take home with them.

- Coloring competition: Have Christmas line drawing blanks of assorted scenes, Santa, Mrs. Claus, Tree, Present, Ornament, Angel, Reindeer, Snow Scene or any other that would fit for the event and a large array of colored crayon markers. Let the children pick out their favorite scene and turn them loose on the markers. The elf in charge of this table should be effusive in praise over how wonderful and creative the artistic efforts of the child. Also make sure the markers stay at the table. A showing of the artistic effort could be arranged by taping the finished "canvas" to the wall for viewing by the parents.

Perhaps the biggest moneymaker for any of these venues would be FACE PAINTING.

First I would warn you to use materials made for use on human skin. Many painters start out using acrylic paints because the colors are so bright and shiny and cheap. The only acrylic paint that does not contain formaldehyde is the Crayola brand of acrylic finger paint and that is not as inexpensive to buy. There are currently 3 types of face paint on the market I am aware of.

The first is Soap based and one manufacturer is Graphtobian Makeup. The second is glycerin based and there are many manufacturers of this type including Mehron, Paradise, Diamond and Wolfe Brothers. The third is basically pancake make-up such as Ben Nye Magic Cake or Star and those are talc-based make-ups. All have their advantages and disadvantages as well as various costs and coverage's per unit. Glitter can be used as long as it is mylorized polyester or mica-based. No craft glitter should ever be used on the face as it is ground metal or glass. Non-metal Metallic type powders such as Ben Nye Lumiere loose eye shadow can also be used with a binder liquid such as liquid set.

Most face painting would be "Cheek Art". A small picture painted on the cheek, forehead, hand or arm. More elaborate half or full face art could also be done. I have found it advantageous to have a "menu" displayed for the children to look at while they wait in line. My menu is a stretched canvas that I have laid out with 4-inch squares using a straight edge and a sharpie pen. Into each square there is a picture sample of what I am doing that day. The child just points at the sample they want and then tells me what colors the want used. This really simplifies and speeds up the process. Here in So Cal a good face painter with experience is paid $75 to $100 an hour by agencies sending them out to parties. Back three years ago when I was still working the area rather than sitting in the mall I paid all the face painters working with me $50 an hour minimum and I supplied the materials.

If you are truly artistic then going out as a Caricature artist elf or Mrs. Claus would be just the thing for a corporate or major event. Agencies here pay $125 to $175 an hour for this type of performer to go to events.

There are many things that you can do to enhance your bottom line and interact in character at Christmas time. These are just a few of the ideas I have worked with or come across over the last 30 years as a professional performing Santa.

SECTION #22: Make-Up And Santa Image Enhancement

From 95 through 2012 I worked in costume shops and helped new Santas with their selections when they came in for suits and helped them with other aspects of their presentation. Theatrical make up was one of those areas I assisted them with. Both the Fun Corner in San Bernardino, California and Harlequin Costume in Ontario, California are full line Ben Nye make-up dealers. Most of the Santas out there can use some help in enhancing their appearance. New (younger) Santas have to cover dark hair and that can be done initially with bleaching which I recommend you go to a professional hair stylist for.

Spot coverage and touch up between bleaching is easily done with theatrical make up. You have several choices to work with. There is Super White Powder for setting creme make-up or you can use Neutral Set if you don't want to go that white. You can apply creme make up with different sized pencils or with a stipple sponge. Then you need to use the powder to "set" it, as creme never dries. Next for touch ups is White Mascara which dries smudge proof (abrasion resistant) and water resistant (won't sweat off). These are easy application and very compact and portable. I use the Mascara to touch up my mustache and eye brows and some Santas use it to color their eye lashes as well.

For larger applications you can use Ben Nye's Snow White liquid hair color. This is made of water, alcohol, glycerin and a dye grit too large to penetrate the hair follicle. You use a brush with bristles like a toothbrush to apply the well shaken liquid to clean dry hair and allow it to dry. The water and the alcohol evaporate and the glycerin holds the dye grit in place. You will need to use a topcoat spray of hair spray to keep the dye grit from rubbing off, as glycerin is not a very strong adhesive.

A different approach is to use hair styling gel (clear) mixed 50% with the Snow White liquid and applied to the hair and combed through. I have seen this done with a Redken styling gel and the result was fantastic. Another choice is the Graphtobian white face paint stick. These are commonly included in the "Santa Kit" the photo company's supply to their set for the Santa. It is basically soap based face paint and will run if made wet (like with sweat).

Traditional bearded Santas use adhesives to hold their beard in place. There again you have several choices. There is spirit gum (which comes in two types, water soluble and non-water soluble) with most using the Matte non water-soluble type. The next step up is Prosthetic Adhesive or Pros-aid, water suspension acrylic co-polymer contact cement. Care must be taken when using Pros-aid. It must be allowed to dry completely clear before allowing the treated prosthetic to come into contact with the coated skin. Otherwise your sweat will cause the adhesive to re-subsume and the piece will fall off and you have to clean up and start over again. Finally there is Medical Adhesive which is a silicone based adhesive with very strong bonding properties.

Before using any adhesive you should clean your skin with soap and water and then use a good astringent like Witch Hazel to give you the best skin contact possible. When removing the piece, use the proper adhesive de-bonder and clean the piece gently to remove any excess adhesive and wash the piece with cleanser to remove any oils before setting it aside to dry before reuse.

The use of a rouge to give you "Rosie cheeks" and a "Nose like a cherry" is also something to consider. You will need to select rouge that works with your skin tone, as unlike hair coloring, one color or style of rouge does not fit all. Use a small round powder brush to apply rouge to the "apple" of your cheeks in a "Nike" swoosh kind of application and just a light spin of the brush to the tip of your nose will do. You can then use a light spray of Ben Nye Final Seal Matte sealer spray to keep it from rubbing off on curious little fingers.

For those with "Oily" complexions, a light dusting of Neutral Set will knock down shine in photographs. Neutral Set looks white but it is actually colorless powder.

Finally you might try a very light application of Ben Nye Opal Ice glitter to your beard. Just a small amount run through your hair and then held in place with a light spray of hair spray will cause tiny highlights to show up in the photo graph. Almost like you had fiber optics woven into your hair. Opal ice is white but gives of a prismatic effect when in the light.

For older Santas there are cover-ups and neutralizers that will make age spots and discolorations fade away if needed. Again the idea is a little bit goes a long way. I recommend you visit a theatrical make up shop and get a consultation on what will help you best by matching what you need to your skin tone. I do not recommend you use street make up as it will not cover as well or last as long, not even Mac. The cost of Ben Nye is about half that of

Mac but the density is about twice that of Mac. "You pay your money and takes your chances."

SECTION #23: What Can A Santa Say To Children?

If you have been playing the role of Santa for any time at all, you are aware of the requests and questions asked by children. Some of these are relatively easy, more in the line of fact checking like:

Q. What are the names of the reindeer?
A. Dasher, Dancer, Prancer, Vixen, Comet, Cupid, Donner, Blitzen and Rudolf.

Q. What are the elves doing?
A. Busy making toys for all the boys and girls and I suspect eating my cookies.

Q. How many elves do you have working for you?
A. Many 1000s of them!

Q. Where is Mrs. Claus?
A. Making cookies at the North Pole with those "Keebler" elves!

Q. What is your favorite cookie?
A. Store bought or homemade? Oreos for store bought and Peanut butter, oatmeal, chocolate chip, walnut, raisin with a sprinkle of cinnamon if homemade!

Then there are the harder questions to answer.

Q. Can you bring me a Puppy for Christmas?
A. A living creature is a very big responsibility! I will have to look into that once I go back to the North Pole. You will have to be very good to receive a puppy for Christmas!

Q. Can I have "Name expensive electronic item here" for Christmas?
A. You have been very good this year! I have a small problem though, when I came down for this visit I checked the inventory in the warehouse and I only had 2 of those left in stock! When I go back up, if there is one left I will put you name on it! Ok?

Q. Can you bring my "relative serving in military" home for Christmas?
A. Well I can try but they are where they need to be right now. I am sure they love you and will be there in their hearts. You could write them a nice letter and send it. They will love to read it and keep it close!

Q. Can you bring my "deceased relative" back to visit for Christmas?
A. I am sorry child, but that is beyond even Santa's powers to grant. God took them to Him and they now reside with Him. Even so, they watch over you and smile.

In many cases you can come up with nice but noncommittal answers. Do not "promise" anything to a child, as the Parents may not be able to purchase it due to budget constraints. Children, while sitting in the chair at the mall, have asked Santa for many things and sometimes the parent will smile and nod at you when the child is focused on you alone asking for that special gift. I have even seen them pull the toy out of a shopping bag behind the child to show me it is in hand. Even then I give qualifications. I tell the child "You have to be good till Christmas! That is only "##" days away!" If they promise to be good I look at the parent and then the child and say, "We will see then. Be good!"

As you can see some questions are very easy and others take some thought and care to answer. Many children simply want to make sure they will not be missed! They will not be home for Christmas because of many different reasons:

- I will be at my Mother's (or Father's) house this year.
- I will be at Grandma's house this year.
- I will be in a Motel
- I will be on the opposite coast.

And the answer is always the same, "Yes the elves will keep the list updated and the list not only tells me if you have been naughty or good, but where to deliver the present!"

Occasionally a child will ask for parents to get back together. To this I answer:

"Your parents love you very much. They simply do not wish to live together right now and that is not your fault. They both want you to be happy and healthy and safe. They both will do everything in their power to make sure that is so but they do not wish to be together. Know that they both love you and hope you love them. Even when they tell you to brush your teeth, do your homework and clean your room they still love you."

There are enough questions to fill a book that come from children. Many are easy to field if you have done your "Santa Lore" homework. Others can be dealt with in humor and common sense. The tough ones take some thought and care for the child's welfare by giving them the knowledge their request to heal a broken home or bring back a dead loved one is beyond the power of Santa but not in any way the fault of the child.

I never tell a child they will receive a particular gift even when the parent has indicated it is in the bag, literally. I always say, "Be good and we will see."

To answer questions better, I suggest you go to the library or book store and pick up a couple of book on the subject of "Cold Reading" and this will help you "seem" more knowledgeable when in fact you are gathering information to feed back to the child.

"Cold reading is the ability to gain information about someone without that person realizing that they are actually giving up the information themselves. This is achieved using a series of tricks and psychological manipulations to coax information out of the interviewee, and then to pass it off as being generated by psychic powers or other means. These tricks are combined with selective reporting or clever editing (of televised readings) to give the appearance that the reading was very successful, and almost magical. If done right, a cold reading leaves a person, or at least most of the audience, completely unaware that they revealed the information themselves."

So in review:
Work to develop your interview skills and practice your responses. Take the time to learn more about the Santa Background story so you can answer the trivia questions. This will make it easier to answer the questions quickly and easily but if you always answer in first person as the answer relates to you as Santa, you will come across much more believable to the children.

SECTION #24: Storytelling By Santa- An Introduction

One of the most valuable skills you can learn as a Santa is that of Storytelling.

Not only is it well received by the audience, both adult and children alike, it also adds another dimension to the Santa character you are portraying. I say dimension because so many new Santa s have very little depth to the character they are playing. I recently gave a lecture and opened with this statement.

"As a new Santa, the more facets or dimensions you bring to the presentation, the greater chance you will be accepted as "Real" by your audience. If your research is limited to the Bass Rankin stop action Claymation movies depicting Santa and life at the North Pole, then you will be a "Claymation, stop action Santa." The more you dig into the character you are playing, the easier it will be for the audience to accept you as a "true" representation of the character you are portraying."

Just so, the more skills you add to your presentation, a knowledge of the history surrounding the character, where the character came from and how it has changed over the last 1700 years since St Nicholas passed away and was canonized, the different traditions surrounding the various Old World characterizations of St Nicholas and the blending of those traditions that eventually came here to America finding a catalyst in Clement C Moore's poem in 1822 that formed the basis of the modern day Santa Claus.

Storytelling is one such way to share those traditions both Old World and New. Storytelling is a skill learned and practiced. My suggestion would be to attend a class, seminar or workshop on Storytelling if possible. But there are ways to make yourself a better Story teller on your own.

If you're going to "Read" a story to a group, make sure you know the story well. Never do a "Cold" reading, as you will be concentrating on the text too much to be able to relate the story well. Storytelling is theater with body and facial language being communicated along with the words you speak.

Practice telling stories by recording them so you can hear what you sound like and improve your cadence. Many people start out mono-toned in their delivery but do not realize it. By recording your telling of the story, you will be able to hear where you need to alter your presentation. You will learn to project your voice and to modulate it to communicate excitement, tension and wonder.

Try to keep your stories short and in keeping in character as you tell them. The telling of "The Night Before Christmas" takes 5 minutes or less. The "Cookie" story only runs 2 to 3 minutes in duration. If you decide to have a "Story Time" segment in your presentation make sure you have your program timed and understand the limits of your audience's attention span.

A typical "Story Segment" that I will perform at home visits will start with "My First Name" which transitions into an explanation of "Traditions" which in turn leads into "The Origin of Santa Claus" which prefaces a telling of "The Night Before Christmas". This ends and the Question comes up about the most famous Reindeer of All and a singing of the song "Rudolf the Red Nosed Reindeer" with a pause after the song to ask the name of the 10th reindeer.

I finish the Story segment with the "Cookie" story.

Santa reads a story

Each of these stories leads from one to the next with programed "Outs" to end the session if circumstances dictate. Some segments are interactive soliciting response from the children such as "My First Name" and the Song singing segment is also audience participation. If you know the time length of each segment, you can pick or choose which segments to use and how they will fit together for each audience to fit the time you have for that portion of your visit. A full "Storytelling" program as part of an hour-long home visit for a single family with 2-4 children will last about 20-25 minutes. It can be made to run shorter simply by cutting any segment you like, as the party needs. By knowing in advance the length of each segment you can craft the "Story Time" to any length you need from 3 minutes to the full 25 and the audience will not notice as your presentation will flow without hesitation. Whatever you do, don't rush! Take your time and just be aware of the time you have and cut the program to the length you need.

When starting out telling stories as Santa, there is a full library to choose from. Some of my favorites are "The Night Before Christmas", "The Polar Express", "The Longest Christmas List", "The Christmas Pumpkin", "Olive the Other Reindeer" along with stories from the adventures of St Nicholas during his works and travels with the Story of "The Three Sisters" a personal favorite.

If doing a Storytelling "visit" I like to leave closing with Robert Frost's poem "Stopping by the Woods on a Snowy Evening" as it makes a great closer.

"The woods are lovely, dark, and deep
But I have promises to keep
And miles to go before I sleep
And miles to go before I sleep."

A few more suggestions would be to keep your storytelling in the first person as much as possible as you are relating stories that "happened" to you or about you as Santa. Most Stories of the genre are relatively short and can be told in 5 minutes or less. The Polar Express is one of the longest but even it can be told in short order without "rushing" the story. Once you have read and memorized the story you are going to tell, try to add some personal touches or comments to it. One of the things I like to share about "The Night Before Christmas" is that it is my favorite story! "Do you know why? It is all about me! If you had a story all about you, it would be your favorite story too!" Keep it in first person, keep it personal and keep it contemporary. Remember to make facial expressions along with arm and hand gestures while telling your story remaining animated in action as well as in voice.

Finally do not be afraid to establish eye contact and hold it with your audience while telling your stories. This helps to "draw" the audience into the world you are trying to create with your story.

Another Storytelling Santa shared that you should ALWAYS give credit to the Author of the story you are telling. This is not only respectful; it will add a little time to the presentation. It is also important to give due credit for using the works of others.

SECTION #25: The Origin Of Santa Claus

This is a preface I give to the story telling segment. It is not a complete history time line as much as it introduces children to the concept of how "Santa" came to be and some of his "Roots" to the "Old World". For a fuller explanation of the development of Santa in the "New World" read the section "Traditions of the "Old World" and how they applied to the "New World" Santa Claus." in this book.

From all over Europe, people came to America starting in the late 1600s through the early 1800s and they brought their traditions with them. During this time America was a largely agrarian based country. People worked the land in one fashion or another Farming, Raising Livestock or Forestry. To be sure there were cities and towns growing and manufacturing and mining as well but by and large they worked the land.

At the winter solstice there is not as much work to be done on a farm as at other times of the year. There were always chores to be done but not so much work. Folks held parties and "get-togethers" during this time when they had an amount of leisure time and they shared their "Old World" traditions of Christmas with their neighbors. The German's with their tradition of the Christmas Tree, The English with their tradition of the Yule Log, The Dutch with their stories of Sinter Klas and Cookies! Oh my, everyone had some sort of cookie or pastry or cake that was special to the season! They also shared their different names of the gift giving person that was a central part of their traditions of Christmas, that is to say St Nicholas. Over time folks from different backgrounds were exposed to other countries traditions and those traditions began to blend and mix.

Then in 1822, a man by the name of Clement C. Moore had a poem published anonymously in a New York newspaper. Everyone was quite taken by the poem and they wanted to know who wrote it and if he had written anything else? Yes the poem was very popular with people buying extra copies! The title of the poem was, "A visit by St. Nicholas" but no one remembered the name. Instead they used the first line of the poem as the title, "Twas the Night Before Christmas".

After handing out candy canes to all that are listening, I then read/recite the story/poem of "The Night Before Christmas". Buy a copy and memorize it! This staple is a classic for the season!

After the telling of the poem, I make a few "incites" and comments on the story in first person as Santa.

"Wasn't that a wonderful story? You know it is my personal favorite! Do you know why? It is all about ME! If you had a story all about you, it would be your favorite to! But it is an important story for 4 reasons:

1. It is the first time they describe me as you see me today!
2. It is the first time they name all 8 of the reindeer!
3. It tells folks how I get in and out of their home while delivering the
4. presents.
5. This is more of a personal pet peeve, but back in 1822, Seventy-one years before the Wright Brother, I am documented flying a "Heavier Than

Air" craft! Do I get credit for that? NO! It is all Orville and Wilbur! And I even gave them their first bicycle!"

As I said, in "The Night Before Christmas" they named all 8 of the reindeer. But does anyone know the name of the 10th reindeer? Rudolf? No he was the 9th reindeer. I will give you a hint. The name of the 10th reindeer is in the song "Rudolf the red nosed reindeer". Let's sing it and see if you can learn the 10th reindeer's name.

At this time I lead the group in singing the song. Once the song has been sung I ask.

Well now, do you know the 10th reindeer's name? [You will hear several suggestions.] No? All right, I will tell you but you're going to groan when you hear it. Here is the 10th reindeer's name. Olive. It was in the song! Don't you remember? Olive, the other reindeer, used to laugh and call him names?
[The song is a nice audience participation portion of the show and a break from telling the stories.]

SECTION #26: Traditions

As St. Nicholas performed many acts of "anonymous giving" over the course of his life, his practice began to spread across the world. Village to town to city after his passing in 343 A D with his elevation to Sainthood, the practice continued to spread in greater number. Someone in a village too ill or injured to work might awaken one morning to find firewood stacked next to gifts of food and clothing. When asked 'Where did these gifts come from and who had given them?' the answer would be "perhaps St. Nicholas brought them." And so the act of 'anonymous giving' spread across the world from Myra (Turkey) to Western Europe and beyond.

Now in different countries there are different traditions and customs just as I have so many different names. From Germany comes the 'Tannembaum' or Christmas Tree. England gave us the 'Yule Log'. Italy brought us 'Ice Wine' and from Holland came cookies.

Other traditions are common throughout Europe. One of the biggest differences between 'Santa' and the Old World 'Father Christmas' is that 'Santa' brings presents while 'Father Christmas' brings judgment. To good little boys and girls, 'Father Christmas' fills their stockings with candy, nuts and fruit. For bad little boys and girls he puts in Coal, bundles of twigs, a raw potato and a pickled egg. The reason for this is, in those countries your

Christmas stocking was your Christmas morning breakfast. Imagine coming down on Christmas morning and seeing your siblings eating candy, nuts and fruit while YOU had to eat a raw potato and a pickled egg!

In Holland there is yet another variation of the 'Stocking' tradition. On Christmas Eve day, the children wear their favorite shoes all day and then leave the shoes by the front door. 'Sinterklass' fills the shoes with the candy, nuts and fruit with some small toys and a coin or two. Some children go to bed very early in anticipation of his arrival. Now I don't know how some 5 year old children wear shoes 3 feet long but they do and 'Sinterklass' keeps his end of the bargain!

Remember my name in Holland? That's right! 'Sinterklass'. Say 'Sinterklass' slowly...sounds like "Santa Claus". Hmmmm...

SECTION #27: My First Name

I always start with this.

What name or names do your know me by?" [The answers usually are] "Santa! Santa Claus! Kris Kringle! Old St Nick!"
[The answers usually slow after this] "Oh I have many names! You probably know me best by "Santa" or Santa Claus" and some of you might know me as Kris Kringle derived from yet another German name "Kristkind" which means "the Christ Child" and of course St. Nick" which comes from St. Nicholas.

In other countries I have different names! In England I am known as 'Father Christmas'. In Germany I am known as 'Father Winter'. In Russia I am known as 'Grandfather Frost'. In France I am called 'Pere Noel' and in Holland they call me 'Sinter Klaws' and I have many more names around the world.

But my first name was Nicholas. Now Nicholas was a real, living person who was born in 280 A.D. and passed away December 6th, 343. That was over 1670 years ago! Coincidentally, that is how old I am. We know of Nicholas because many of his deeds and works were documented and recorded back then.

Nicholas was born to a couple late in their life. He was not expected but he was loved and cherished by his parents. His parents were merchants and in those times they had to travel to buy and sell their wares. One day on such a trip, they became ill and died, leaving Nicholas an orphan. So monks raised Nicholas in an orphanage. Nicholas was so impressed by how the monks treated the children under their care, he decided to become a monk himself and so became the youngest monk of his order.

Now as a monk, Nicholas lived and worked in a monastery that was in the land of Myra, which we now call Turkey today. A monastery is a large building with a sturdy wall that surrounds it on all 4 sides. The monks worked in the nearby town and surrounding farms and orchards. (For those of you that don't know what a monk is, a monk is a religious person like a minister or a priest but instead of giving sermons in a church, monks worked side by side with the people of the lands and town they lived near. There are Monk bakers, and monk candle makers, and monk wine makers and monk farmers) and as they worked they spread the word of God.

The monastery was where you went to learn your letters and numbers. If you were injured or sick, you would go to the monastery to be made whole and well. Because of the large building and strong walls surrounding it, the monastery was a place of shelter and safe haven in times of strife. The Guild Masters and Town Leaders liked having all the benefits of the monastery nearby but they did not like their workers distracted by talk of religion. So they passed a law stating no one should speak of religious matters unless within the confines of 4 walls. Thinking that would keep the benefits of having the monastery nearby without any distractions from the monks.

Nicholas did not like this new law! He wanted to talk to anyone anytime about anything, much like any of you I suspect. So Nicholas spent an entire summer sewing up bags and into these bags he placed dried fruit, nuts, honeycomb, dried flowers and a few coins. Then at the winter solstice, Nicholas would knock on doors and whoever answered the door, Nicholas would give the gift of a bag.

Now in the middle of winter in that part of the world back then, food was very scarce so the dried fruit, nuts and honeycomb were greatly appreciated! The dried flowers remind them of the coming of spring and so gave a message of hope. Of course the coins were always appreciated, but it was the bag itself that was the most highly prized item! Do you know why? Back then, pockets had not been invented yet! If you went to market to buy or sell something, you had to carry it in your hands, put it in your hat, or if you had a bag you could carry much more!"

So overwhelmed by the gift of the bag, people would invite Nicholas inside and there within the confines of 4 walls, he could talk about anything he chose. Thus Nicholas spread the word of God. Now Nicholas lived a long life spanning 63 years with many accomplishments and adventures. He became the "Boy Bishop" and helped many people along the way of his life. When at last Nicholas passed away he was canonized. (Do you know what that means? They shot him out of a canon! ... NO! They made him a Saint!) And so Nicholas became St. Nicholas and that became my first name!

That is also why Santa has no pockets in his suit and why Santa always carries a bag,

SECTION #28:   The Elves, Mrs. Claus And Treats

Now before I tell you this story, there are 2 things you need to know. First, the youngest elf at the North Pole working in the Toy Shop is over 175 years old! Now that is very young for an Elf but very old for a human. Secondly, I don't know the rule in your home but at the North Pole, if you bite into a cookie…. You have to finish it! Not my rule, Mrs. Claus does not like having half eaten treats sitting around where I might gobble them up.

Now most likely you have not heard this story before because it only happened recently. We had a small problem at the North Pole. You see, the Elves stopped eating their vegetables! They only wanted to eat cookies, pies, cakes and candy. While this did give the Elves a 'Sugar Rush' and spiked production for a while, there were some drawbacks to this behavior of the Elves. You see, when you're over 175 years old and you stop eating your vegetables, you get a little cranky. Not a good thing!

So Mrs. Claus and I put our heads together and tried to come up with a solution. And Mrs. Claus came up with the answer! She baked vegetables into the cookies! Have you ever had a Peanut Butter, Oatmeal, Chocolate Chip, Lima Bean, Brussels Sprout cookie? Well they are kind of chewy! Ecccuuuuwww!   Have you ever tried one? No? Well you can't say "Eeeeuuuuwww" then, can you?

Now remember the rule? Bite into a cookie and you have to finish it? Well, Mrs. Claus put a BIG platter of those Peanut Butter, Oatmeal, Chocolate chip, Lima Bean; Brussels Sprout cookies out on that day and the Elves simply pounced on them! Almost at once, we had a lot of Elves going around with their cheeks puffed out like chipmunks and we went through a LOT of milk that day!

Santa & Mrs. Claus

But then the Elves stopped eating the cookies, so Mrs. Claus whipped up a delightful batch of Double Chocolate Fudge, Walnut, and Asparagus brownies! After that, the Elves decided to start eating their vegetables so they could enjoy their treats the normal way, without the vegetables. But I kind of got used to those Peanut Butter, Oatmeal, Chocolate Chip, Lima Bean, and Brussels Sprout cookies, so Mrs. Claus makes me a batch every now and then.

SECTION #29: Mrs. Claus

Sometimes an adult will be reluctant to sit on Santa's knee. "I am too heavy" is often used as an excuse. This story will give your adults a chuckle and ease them onto your knee for that picture.

You're too heavy? Why next to Mrs. Claus your light as a feather! Now when I first met Mrs. Claus she was what you would call today a "Hottie" as she weighed only 115 pounds. I have always looked like what you see me as today but this young lady saw something in me she wanted to go after and so she pursued my affections relentlessly until finally I gave in and consented to be married. Now I love Mrs. Claus dearly and we had a very good and stable relationship throughout our time together, but I really had the better end of the deal as far as I could see!

You see, Mrs. Claus turned out to be the BEST cookie maker ever! She spends All her waking hours in the kitchen baking cookies when she isn't helping organizing the Elves or getting me ready for my ride around the world. Oh, the variety and flavors she makes are endless! However, Mrs. Claus is a "taster" in the kitchen and she has gained a little weight.

Now in her defense, Mrs. Claus only gained 1 pound a year! And a stable and mutually respectable marriage partnership is not based on looks alone. God knows I love Mrs. Claus for who she is but the cookies are a nice bonus indeed! Of course we have been married over 800 years now..."

So that is why I say 'Next to Mrs. Claus your light as a feather! Ho Ho Ho!

SECTION #30: The Export Of Santa To Other Countries

I have many online friends from other countries – some through social media and others through MMRPG interaction. Fallen Sword is one such game that incorporates real time conversations around the world with other players and it can be an eye opener of how life is outside the US. One such friend is a Belgium Navy Marine Noncom that has been in the service for a long time. He is nearing his retirement from the Belgium Marines and I have been carrying on conversations with him for the last 3 years. His game handle is "navy cop" and here are a few statements he has made about the contrasts of St Nicholas to Santa and how he sees the importation of Santa into his country and the way it has supplanted St Nicholas there.

"Navy cop says: Since the US wants us to stop with St Nicolas cause his helper being black (all though I can't see where they call it racism, cause he's a white man being black from climbing down chimneys) it might very well be within a few years we have a Santa instead of St Nicolas."

Please note I believe navy cop is talking about the recent UN attempt to alter the use of Black Pete, not the US.

The following is a personal timeline account of how Santa has come to Belgium.

"Navy cop says: To my opinion: In a few years St Nick will be replaced by Santa. When I was a child all we knew was St Nic. Santa was unknown to us. When I was a teenager, Santa was introduced when the BBC came to our TV. As a twin Santa became a known figure due to movies. In my thirties it started to get promoted in shops, but St Nick was still in our minds on Dec 6th and Santa on Dec 25th along with the Christmas tree. Now days even at work, they replaced St Nick with Santa. So in a few years, St Nick will be forgotten all together."

In the next snippet navy cop gives a little background in the local traditions and story line.

"Navy cop says: Here St Nick comes to the Netherlands and Belgium to gives a speech on a balcony. In his speech he says there are no naughty children this year, but then he says that every year, LOL. Then he finishes saying there will be presents for all children. I don't see any difference between Santa and St Nick in that. Real story says St Nick was a bad lumberjack who came along stealing naughty children in the past. Since they wanted to keep the story but change his character, he became a good man giving children that were good presents. I saw the movie of St Nick a short while ago and I can tell you he really wasn't a good person. Now for his helpers, in the movie those were "white" guys (mostly the people he had captured previously) they went down the chimney to get more bad people (reason of their black color). The fuzz was they looked too much like (pardon the language) "Negroes", cause they were black, had red lips and curly hair. I can see the resemblance, but in no way that was intended. Loosing Black Peter, to us, would be like ditching the elves the helpers of Santa. (All the Black Peter's help making the presents for the children) St Nick on its own has almost no meaning without Black Peter. Now this might seem hard, but to me it's sort of a campaign to ditch St Nick and replacing him with Santa. If Santa is promoted more often and St Nick gets forgotten, more advertisements can come over to Europe from the states or other countries. What really is the big picture in all this (but this is only my opinion)"

Of course navy cop recognizes the commercial side of Santa being inserted into his culture.

"Navy cop says: To us St Nick is (nowadays) in no way a bad person. He is a bringer of gifts for children of all ages (yeah, even some grown-ups get presents on December 6th, St Nick's day). Even Black Peter now is a bringer of cookies, candy and chocolates. He's a bit scary at first for the very small children, but once they start seeing him passing out candy and cookies, they soon melt away for the guy. We had 8 children and none of them ever thought of him being a "real black" person, but like someone who went down the chimes. Now I can imagine some little ones being scared of Santa too when they first meet, even scared of an elf, LOL. I just can't see any reason to exchange Saint Nick by Santa. Why can't they both continue doing their good works? We don't mind taking St Nick and Santa both since the first is December 6th and the second only comes on Christmas."

They even have their version of a "Bad Santa" Movie and navy cop was kind enough to send me a link to it for folks to look up.
http://kickass.to/sint-2011-720p-bluray-mkv-x264-dts-ee... (You can download the movie here, it's a torrent)
http://www.imdb.com/title/tt1167675/

This is given with navy cop's permission and it illustrates not every culture is like what is here in the US and should be considered when accepting an overseas job posting.

SECTION #31: Live Appearances Of Santa In America – A Timeline

It began as a new idea in a new country. St Nicholas was brought to the New World and first mentioned in print in 1773. Referred to as St. A Claus in the New York Gazette. Still referred to as St Nicholas in most cases, this is the beginning of a name change. (www.christmas....org/santa.html)

Through the writings of Washington Irving, as "Diedrich Knickerbocker," in 1809 with the Knickerbocker Papers, then with the publishing of " A New Year's Present for the Little Ones from Five to Twelve" in 1821 by William B. Gilley of New York, followed closely by "An Account of a Visit from St. Nicholas." in 1822 which is credited to Clement C. Moore who was a friend and neighbor of William Gilley. These three publishing's set the image of Santa Claus in America. (www.stnichola...orgin-of-santa/)

In 1804, John Pintard is credited with bringing the first mass produced images of a Santa like setting. He had a series of woodcuts he had distributed to fellow members of the New York Historical Society's annual meeting. (www.history,c....ics/santa-claus)

The next really influential artist to further define the image of Santa Claus was Thomas Nast with his first published drawing in Harper's Weekly newspapers back in Christmas Eve 1862 but distributed in Jan of 1863. In a picture that sides with the Union Santa is seen in a sleigh pulled by Reindeer in a "Stars & Bars" Santa suit that has many features common to modern day Santa. (www.sonofthes....SantaClaus.htm)

In 1915 we see Santa driving a truck delivering White Rock soda water and flying a Bi-plane in 1916 again delivering White Rock product. Santa kept up with technological advancements in many fields! (www.whiterocking.org/santa.html)

While the first pictures of Santa promoting Coca Cola were used in the 1920's depicting a stern looking Nast like presentation of Santa, it is Haddon Sundblom that is given credit to the iconic "Coca Cola Santa" look. Sundblom's first rendering was in 1931 with an ad titled "My hat's off to the pause that refreshes". Haddon Sundblom painted his final image of Santa Claus for Coca Cola in 1964. During that span Sundblom created several variations to the "Santa" image including using brown belt and boots to shift to black belt and boots, he also did a version of a "Work shop Santa" with the red coat off and his sleeves rolled up. (www.coca-cola.uk/)

The first Department store Santa was Jim Edgar, the owner of The Boston Store, dressed in a Santa suit and started to ask children what they wanted for Christmas, starting a new American tradition of personal interviews with Santa! He did not start out sitting in a chair; instead Jim Edgar would walk around in his store and talk to children as he encountered them. This began in the Christmas season of 1890. Before Jim Edgar there were life sized Santa figures in stores but until he put the Red Suit on, there was no "live" Santa to visit. (www.firstdepartime...emagarticle.pdf)

Then it quickly followed that the Salvation Army took a number of unemployed men and placed them in Santa suits to solicit donations to help pay for the holiday meals the SA provided. That practice began in 1891, the year following Jim Edgar's example of a live presentation of Santa. (www.history.c...ics/santa-claus)

In 1937 the first "Santa School" came into being taught by Charles W. Howard. Running continuously every year for 3 days since the CWH Santa School is the oldest and longest running school for Santas. (www.santaclau...com/about.html)

Established in 1983 is the Professional Santa Claus School of Denver. Starting on a Friday evening and finishing on a Tuesday morning, the PSCS of Denver is one of the longest session schools as well as the second longest running. (www.amerevent...a-claus-school/)

Starting out in 2003 but running nearly year round is the International University of Santa Claus (IUSC). The very first class was given on the campus of USC in the Geriatric Hall (kind of fitting when you think about it). Owned and operated by Santa Tim Connaghan, aka: Santa Hollywood a professional Santa with over 45 years of experience. This school has grown and developed to cover 2 days of information workshop modules filled with power point visuals and lectures. This is a "traveling" school that covers many locations across the country and on the Seas! (www.realsantas.com/iusc.htm)

One of the newest schools to teach Santas is the St. Nicholas Institute. This is a three-day educational retreat, which splits the focus on both Santa and St Nicholas. Very informative and well worth the cost to attend!

I would also add this book, Santa and the Business of Being Santa, and the Santa School by the same name as a place to learn much about the history, workings and education of Santas. I am sure there are more Santa Schools than mentioned in this chapter and more are starting every year.

So you see the tradition of Santa Claus is still very much in the formative state with less than 150 years of live presentation to the general public. Starting out as a shift away from the "Old World" traditions and having a "hay day" as advertising tool for all manner of product, Santa is beginning to find his home and traditions even today. In the footnotes I have left the Internet addresses for the sources I used to find this information. Simply by using them as a starting point you can begin your own voyage of discovery.

SECTION #32: The Changing Image And Traditions Surrounding Santa Claus As Opposed To St. Nicholas And "Old World" Traditions

St Nicholas was a real living person of history that was documented in record. Many of his actions and deeds are the basis of our Christmas traditions. From St Nicholas's time to the late 1700's there were numerous traditions with a central figure based upon St Nicholas and each had very special stories and traditions linked to that character. Father Christmas, Father Winter, Grandfather Frost, Sinter Claus and many, many more.

In the 1700's and early 1800's many people immigrated to America and they brought their traditions with them. As they generally celebrated at Christmas time and the Winter Solstice, they would invite their friends and neighbors to join in their celebrations. Thus the various traditions were blended and mixed.

The Knickerbocker Papers were the first written mention of a character that resembles the modern day Santa. Then after several other publications followed suit, Clement C. Moore wrote his poem "A visit from St. Nicholas" in 1822. No one remembered the name of the story, they referred to it by the first line "Twas the Night Before Christmas" and that firmly "fixed" the image of the modern day Santa since that time on.

The image was further defined and refined first by Thomas Nast, 1872 and then further by Haddon Hubbard "Sunny" Sundblom (June 22, 1899 – March 10, 1976) an artist best known for the images of Santa Claus he created for The Coca-Cola Company.

While based upon the various traditions of St Nicholas from many countries, "Santa Claus" is and remains a totally American invention and is now being exported to the rest of the world. Santa Claus has been used to advertise products ranging from cigarettes, pipes and tobacco to shaving items to watches and jewelry to foodstuffs and soda pop to vehicles and even to promote supporting the troops during times at war dating back to the American Civil War through the Vietnam conflict. Santa has promoted all manner of commercial item and has been sitting in Stores and Malls to listen to the wishes and desires of Children of all ages.

While "Santa" may have started out as an advertising tool in the later part of the 1860's through to today, the image and character of "Santa" is still changing and maturing along with the traditions surrounding his appearance. Many movies being made in the last century and the last 13 years have added to this change in traditions and are part of why the traditions surrounding Santa have changed so rapidly in comparison to those that formed in the "old World".

The most prominent shift from "Old World" to "New" is the basic concept of a visit from Santa. Father Christmas, Father Winter, Grandfather Frost et al were more in the idea of bringing "judgment". To good children he brought candy, nuts, fruit, a few coins and perhaps a small gift or two usually left on the table, in a stocking or shoe. Bad children received lumps of coal, a raw potato, pickled egg and perhaps a bundle of twigs or sticks known as a "faggot" usually used to start a fire. This practice of "judgment" varied from country to country as did St Nicholas's mode of transportation and companions.

The tradition of Santa has always been one of the gift giver of love and forgiveness. This tradition has roots in the St Nicholas traditions but has become a focus of the character in main part.

Santa Gordon Bailey

Lately in the last 15 years a movement to shift the concept of "Santa" towards that of a more "Old World" tradition of St. Nicholas has been becoming a popular concept for those more interested in the deeper religious influences while others are striving to make their presentation based upon the drawing of Nast including the "Stars & Bars" Santa that was drawn to promote the Union effort in the War between the States. The inclusion of religious crosses and the influence of the Sundblom "Coca Cola" Santa suit have also been added to the mix.

Where once a character used to celebrate the season generally starting to make his appearance from "Black Friday" through New Year's Day, now Santa is involved in Malls starting as early as October, seen in amusement parks year round and increasingly involved in "Care & Comfort" visits year round to disaster locations in the United States. The "Convoy of Toys" started by the Lone Star Santa group has influenced several other groups to start their own programs of a similar nature. Santa America has been working with hospice groups providing Santa visits year round for about a decade now. All of these activities are a distinct break form Father Christmas sitting in his Grotto waiting for visitors.

The image of Santa is changing constantly as the role is expanded to meet new challenges. It will remain an "Image in Flux" as long as new interpretations and traditions continue to be developed. As recent developments have shown, while the image of the "Home visit Santa" and the definition of the "Mall Santa" have pretty much jelled, the total concept of "Santa" has yet to be reached and there will be new Ideas, new concepts and images and "jobs" for Santa coming in the future. In a very real sense of the word, Santa is what you make of him for some time to come.

SECTION #33: How Traditions Of The Old World And New World Are Applied To Santa Claus

Krampus, Black Peter or Black Pete even the Devil is part of the entourage that accompanies Father Christmas or Father Winter around some European countries in their traditions. While they do not play an "Evil" role in the Christmas traditions, they are part of the "Judgment" placed upon the children to determine if they have been good or naughty.

You see, in the "Old World" traditions, stress was placed upon the judgment of whether the children had been "Naughty" or "Nice". This judgment was brought by Father Christmas mainly in the form of the "gifts" he would bring to them. Depending on the country of origin, St Nicholas would have various means of transportation and a wide variety of companions as well.

Generally on the night St Nicholas would visit, his "gifts" for good children would be candies, fruit, edibles and perhaps a small gift or toy and also perhaps a coin or two depending on the traditions of the host "Old World" country. Bad children would receive coal, bundles of twigs, a pickled egg, a raw potato and the like. Primarily the Christmas stocking was your Christmas breakfast. Imagine coming down to see your siblings eating candy, nuts, fruit, cookies and cakes while you had to eat a pickled egg and a raw potato. Instead of a toy or coins you had something to burn to stay warm. In both cases the child's welfare was looked after but the way it was presented to the child indicated how they had been judged.

In America, the "New World", Santa Claus brought large gifts of toys and clothes along with the candy, fruit, nuts and various stocking stuffers. The "Judgment was in large part left behind in the "Old World" with the vestige carryover of the "Naughty or Nice" list and the distant possibility of receiving a lump of coal. Modern day Santa is seen bringing Presents, Joy, Love and the promise of Hope.

The following are a few of the "companion" traditions and what was done to scare children or nudge them toward being good:

"Svatý Mikuláš, the Czech St. Nick, is usually dressed in the white robes of bishop. Accompanied by an angel and a devil, Svatý Mikuláš brings gifts to children on the Eve of St. Nicholas, which is observed on December 5. The angel is the good children's representative; the devil the bad children's representative. If you're visiting Prague or another city in the Czech Republic on this day, you may see St. Nicholas and his companions on their way to bestow gifts upon children. This cool Santa may accept a drink from parents once his duties are through."

"As it was explained to me, this visit happens 10 days before Christmas. When the trio comes to the home, the parents get to tell how bad the children were all year (or how good) and then after hearing this evidence, the child is allowed to give a defense explaining any and all misunderstandings."

"The three visitors then confer and render their judgment by giving the child a golden coin for being good or a potato or lump of coal for being bad. The child then has to go around the neighborhood and show what they received to the other children in the area."

This does 2 things. First it gives them 10 days to get into the good graces of Svatý Mikuláš before the "big visit" on Christmas Eve. Second, peer pressure is a wonderful device to help children modify their behavior. Everyone wants to be seen as being "good".

Likewise we have Black Peter who also has several names.

"Zwarte Piet (pronounced [ˈzʋartə pit], "Black Pete"; French: Père Fouettard [pɛʁ fwɛtaʁ], "Father Whip") is a companion of Saint Nicholas (Dutch: Sinterklaas) in the folklore of the Low Countries, whose yearly feast in the Netherlands is usually celebrated on the evening of 5 December (Sinterklaasavond, that is, St. Nicholas' Eve) and 6 December in Belgium, when they distribute sweets and presents to all good children.

The characters of Zwarte Pieten appear only in the weeks before Saint Nicholas's feast, first when the saint is welcomed with a parade as he arrives in the country (generally by boat, having traveled from Madrid, Spain). The tasks of the Zwarte Pieten are mostly to amuse children, and to scatter pepernoten, kruidnoten and strooigoed (special sinterklaas candies) for those who come to meet the saint as he visits stores, schools, and other places.

The original Zwarte Piet is sometimes associated with Knecht Ruprecht, but in the Low Countries the tradition has not merged with Christmas."

This character has always been associated with St Nicholas in the Netherlands as someone that beats bad children with sticks and then stuffs them into a bag to take them far away.

According to myths dating to the beginning of the 19th century, Saint Nicholas operated by himself or in the companionship of a devil. Having triumphed over evil, it was said that on Saint Nicholas Eve the devil was shackled and made his slave; a devil as a helper of the saint can still be found in the Austrian Saint Nicholas tradition, in the character of Krampus.

Some sources indicate that in Germanic Europe, Zwarte Piet was originally such an enslaved devil, forced to assist his captor, but in the 19th century Netherlands the character emerged in the likeness of a Moor, a servant of Saint Nicholas. Saint Nicholas is said to come from the Byzantine Empire, modern-day Turkey.

The introduction of this new Zwarte Piet was paired with a change in the attitude of the Sinterklaas character, who became quite severe towards bad children himself, and worried teachers and priests due to the depiction of a holy man in this light. Sometime after the introduction of Zwarte Piet as Sinterklaas' servant, both characters adapted a softer character.

Still, the lyrics of older traditional Sinterklaas songs warn that while Sinterklaas and his assistant will leave well-behaved children presents, they will punish those who have been very naughty. For example, they will take bad children and carry these children off in a burlap sack to their homeland of Spain, where, according to legend, Sinterklaas and his helper dwell out of season. **"These songs and stories also warn that a child who has been only slightly naughty will not get a present, but a "roe", which is a bundle of birch s and twigs, implying that they could**

have gotten a birching instead, or they will simply receive a lump of coal instead of gifts."

As you can see, the modern day Santa Claus traditions and stories have a lot in common with those of Sinterklaas. In many trains of thought the name Sinterklaas is credited for the name Santa Claus. Sinter Klaas - Santa Claus. They are very similar in phonetic sounding.

There are as many different traditions for the "Old World" St Nicholas as there are countries that hold them. Just as there are different names such as Father Christmas, Father Winter, Grandfather Frost, and Pere Noel and on and on. There are many names for St. Nicholas and they all have wonderful traditions. Santa Claus is formed from a combination of those "Old World" Traditions into something entirely new.

Santa is an American invention dating from the early 1800s beginning with the Knickerbocker papers and continuing through to a more solidly "gelled" concept in 1823 with the poem "A Visit from St. Nicholas" credited to Clement C. Moore.

Further given definition through the artwork of Thomas Nast. Nast first drew Santa Claus for the 1862 Christmas season Harper's Weekly cover and center-fold illustration to memorialize the family sacrifices of the Union during the early and, for the north, darkest days of the Civil War. This is where we first see the "Stars and Bars" Santa suit depicted.

Then further on through the work of Haddon Hubbard "Sunny" Sundblom (June 22, 1899 – March 10, 1976) an artist best known for the images of Santa Claus he created for The Coca-Cola Company. Santa has been an advertising figure used to sell things from shaving soap to razors, bb guns to cars, cigarettes to pipe tobacco, soft drinks to hard liquor, and to jewelry and house hold appliances to mention a few.

To explain and describe all of the variations upon the Father Christmas theme and the traditions surrounding him from the many countries would take a book with 1000s of pages. The best I can suggest to you if you're interested enough to learn more about the "Back story" of where Santa came from would be to Google St Nicholas, Father Christmas and Christmas Around The World to start. By no means is this the complete study guide as there is far more information out there to learn. It will give you a good basic start on Christmas traditions from around the world and you will begin to see how Santa has his roots in many different cultures.

As I see it, Santa Claus is a young tradition and still in the process of being defined. I believe this process will continue for decades if not centuries yet to come. Already the idea and character of Santa has begun to be exported to many countries around the world supplementing and in some cases substituting the original traditions that have been there for centuries. You now see Santa Claus being employed in China, Japan, the Philippines, India, Asia, Russia, England and the UK, Spain and France and the Netherlands, Canada and Mexico. In fact around the world the name "Santa Claus" is becoming more and wider spread in recognition since 1940 and the trend will continue.

SECTION #34: Personal Encounters

PERSONAL ENCOUNTERS:
A TYPICAL ENCOUNTER ON A TYPICAL DAY

I was waiting at Staples today for some printing work to be finished. Visual aids for a lecture I do and some new business cards. A small boy came up to the same counter I was waiting at and began to act out just the slightest bit with his Mom standing right behind him.

He looked at me, (I was dressed all in black from head to toe) and then continued to be a small boy. You know, eyes in the fingers, etc. He was totally ignoring his mother and I could see she was a little tired so I started up a conversation with the lad as I waited.

As the Mother watched carefully our conversation went like this:

M: Hello, how are you today?
LB: I am good!
M: How old are you?
LB: I am 6!
M: Oh! You're an old man!

LB:	No I'm not!
M:	Oh yes! It is all downhill after 5! (At this point Mom starts to smile)
LB:	How come?
M:	One of life's cruel jokes! You spend the first 5 years of your life getting teeth in your head and then they start to fall out! Lose any teeth lately?
LB:	Smiles to show a gap and then asked, who are you?
M:	I am old.
LB:	What do you do?
M:	A lot of things, mostly I talk to people.
LB:	Oh.
M:	Is that your girlfriend? (Indicating the Mother)
LB:	NO!
M:	Bodyguard?
LB:	Yeah, sometimes you could say she is my Bodyguard. (Mom starts to chuckle.)
M:	Is she your Girlfriend inspector?
LB:	NO!
M:	Wanna bet? You bring a girlfriend home and she is going to inspect it real good! In fact I can tell you exactly what she will say.
LB:	Really, what? (Mom is really listening now)
M:	She will look her over real good then she will say "Sniff! Not good enough!"
LB:	(looking up at Mom) Really?
	Mom: (Laughing) Yes!
M:	I know these things; I had a girlfriend inspector once.
LB:	Can you do magic?
M:	Sometimes. It depends on what I have to do.
LB:	Can you make me disappear?
M:	No, because then your Mom could not see you to feed you.

While I am carrying on this conversation I show the mother some pics of me performing on my phone.

LB: do some magic!
M: Alright, but first what is that? (Pointing at his shirt.)
LB: What? My shirt?
M: No, that! (Still pointing)
LB: Spider-man? (Pointing at the picture on the shirt)
M: No, this! (Having palmed my squeaker, I squeak his tummy)
LB: WHAAAT?!? Mom! Did you see that? (Mom is laughing again)
M: Do you always do that?
LB: No. How did you do that?
M: I am old; I am good at finding squeaky spots.
LB: Do it again!
M: Well, I guess so… (Proceed to squeak the boy in the same place again) (Mom is really laughing now)
M: (to mom) this is what I do, I bring a little surreal into their lives.
LB: Do something else! Do more magic!
M: Did you wash behind your ears today? (Palming the dollar coin in my pocket)
LB: No. Why?
M: You have something growing out of your ear.
LB: (grabbing his ear) What!!??
M: Let me get it for you. (Reach out w/ palmed coin and pull it out of his ear.)
LB: (Eyes get wide!) Mom! Did you see that? Do it again!!
M: Well I pretty much cleaned that ear out.
LB: Can I have it?
M: Nope! Finders, Keepers. (Noticing a dime on the floor behind him)

LB:	How about the other ear?
M:	(Reaching out with the palmed coin once again) Yup! There is another one! Thanks Kid!
LB:	I never find any money.
M:	Turn around and look down.
LB:	(Turns around and finds the dime I noticed earlier) Wow! You're good!
M:	You keep that. Finders, Keepers.
LB:	Can you do anything else?
M:	Well when my powers are up I can do a lot.
LB:	ARE YOU SANTA?
M:	Does Santa wear all black?
LB:	Well, no, I guess not.
M:	(While he was looking down I pulled my beard out of my shirt) Want to know a little secret? (Mom is really smiling now)
LB:	What?
M:	(In a very quiet voice) I am Santa... have you been good?
LB:	I KNEW IT! MOM! Mom: Santa does check up on children, see?
LB:	I am being good!

About then the lady's order was ready and they had to go pick up Dad. The little boy was very happy and said goodbye and the mother said thank you.

The Printer service girl said, "I can see from the photos what you do but if what you just did is any indication of the act you do, you are really great!" I thanked her for the compliment and paid for my printing that only took 3.5 hours to complete and went home.

That was how part of my day went, how was yours?

PERSONAL ENCOUNTERS:
AND THE BLIND SHALL SEE

Today I was visited by a young lady who had never sat on Santa's knee before. At the ripe old age of 9, this young lady had never had the pleasure of seeing Santa personally. Today was that day!

This little girl was blind and did not know what to expect when she sat on my knee. The Mother was somewhat anxious and apologetic while she explained her daughter was blind and had never sat with Santa before. I ask if she would like to "see" me. The Mom was somewhat surprised at my willingness to have the girl touch my face and beard to "see" what I looked like. Once we began the girl was a little cautious but as she discovered different textures in my beard and hair, she became more confident. The glasses were next and then she had to feel the velvet and fur of my suit. Next came the boots, belt and last came the gloves.

I wear band gloves with rubber gripper dots on the palms and fingers to have a more secure grip. The little girl asked me what the gloves were saying. Her Mother was a bit confused by that and I explained why I had the bumpy feel to my gloves and how they made sure I could maintain a good grip gently so children in my care would be safe. The little girl said "That is nice of you to think of that."

After having been thoroughly examined and concluded the interview, I gave the girl a book but it was not in braille and she could not read it. The Mother saw my dismay at this and said to her daughter that she would have it "brailed" as soon as she got home. I think if I have more children with sight impairment visiting me this year, next year I will look into having some books in Braille handy for them as giveaways. Both Santa and the little girl learned something with this visit!

Remember to be childlike, never childish when dealing with children as Santa. I took a little bit more time to deal with the situation but the little girl, her mother and the people that were with the group were very happy with the photos that were taken. The smile on the little girl's face was well worth the effort and time to let her "see" me.

May your season be Joyous and prosperous.

PERSONAL ENCOUNTERS: MORE FUN AT THE MALL FOR SOME

I have been at the same mall now for 3 years and have developed a sort of following with regular visitors. Some of these are mentally developed in different ways; others are physically different in their abilities. All of them love to visit with Santa and give very enthusiastic hugs! Last year the company I work for had a special pricing of $5 for a photo as a celebration of their 20 years in the business. This year the least expensive is $16.99 and with tax comes in at $18.35 for a single 5x7. I had a group of 4 ladies that wanted to have a picture with Santa but did not have the means to pay.

I am allowed a 5x7 photo for working as Santa on the set and so I used my photo to give the ladies what they so badly wanted. You see, 46% of all the people living in this city are receiving some form of assistance. These are very hard times for many of those that live in San Bernardino and I very much want to give hope and joy to as many I can while I perform as Santa.

This is a good thing yet I have limited resources and as the season rolls on more demands upon my time.

While I had just one free picture to do what I wished with, I have had many people asking for help in many instances. There was ONE big exception that stands out in my mind. A 12-year-old girl came to visit with me last week. She was well-dressed and obviously well cared for with a happy smile on her face and no big demands or wishes. Her mother was a bit worn looking but obviously loved her daughter. What is so special about this little girl? She is in a wheel chair and she zips along with this big happy smile every time I see her in the mall. Her last visit, Mom lifted her from her chair and set her down on my knee to have another chat but this time it was just like all the other children, sitting on Santa's knee rather than sitting in her chair and I sitting in mine.

I finished the interview and asked the Mom if they were going to take a picture today? The Mother looked a little pained and said "I don't have the money" and the little girl was putting a brave face on it by saying, "That's alright, I got to sit on your knee." I thought about it for maybe 30 seconds and called the photographer over and quietly told him to take a picture for the little girl and to tell the manager that I would take care of the cost.

The Mother was surprised and the little girl seemed delighted! I figured I didn't really need to have lunch that day as my suit was a bit snug anyway. Skipped dinner too but it was worth it. Now that child has her picture and I am a little slimmer. Win/Win! I wish I could do this with every one of my "special" friends but unfortunately I can't. This must remain a rare and occasional indulgence for when my budget allows or my suit gets too snug.

SOME VISITS ARE FUN, SOME ARE SAD, THIS ONE MADE ME CRY

I have been busy all day today on this first Saturday of December. Lots of hugs and wishes listened to and photos taken. Many, many happy faces sitting on my lap telling me what they desire most for Christmas.

Then a little 6-year-old girl sits down and says "All I want for Christmas is to have my mother share it with me at home". Small warning bells are going off in my head as I look up to see both her mother and Grandmother standing by the photographer watching while we are being photographed. I ask the little girl "Where is your mother right now?" and the little girl points at the woman I thought was the Mom. I then asked, "Where will you be staying on Christmas?" thinking maybe they were going away somewhere but the little girl replies "With my Dad and Grandma". Now I am stumped but think maybe this is a broken home situation until the girl tells me her mother will be in Afghanistan during Christmas! Now I am TOTALLY out to sea without a paddle or a compass!

I finished the photo session with the little girl and gave her a book and told her to go look at the pictures we just took. Then I called the Mom over to talk to her. I tell Mom the request of the little girl and the Mom explains she is a Navy Medic that will be going on deployment next Wed and she won't be around on Christmas. A little light is shining through but I continue to ask questions and find out Mom will be serving with an ARMY detachment as their medic. I said "ARMY? I knew the NAVY provided medics for the MARINES but ARMY too?" Mom sighed and said yes this was something new and she had been given 2 weeks leave before being deployed attached to an ARMY unit. That made me think harder and faster!

I let Mom go to be with her daughter for a few minutes while they finished their transaction and then called the Mom back for a last consult. I told her of my many friends in the service that used Skype with video to stay in touch with family at home and Mom said she had just had it set up that day and taught her mother (Grandma) and daughter how to use it. I then told Mom she could go to Hallmark and purchase one of their recordable storybooks and read the story and then leave it as a Christmas present for her daughter. That way when her daughter was home and missing mom, she could hear mom reading her a story. Mom looked very surprised and then happy while crying at the same time and said "I am going to get one or two of those right now!" Now I wish there were something more I could do but my powers as Santa are extremely limited to holding hands and telling stories while listening to wishes. I thanked Mom for her service, told her to be careful and to keep faith. After they left, I had to take a minute to get something out of my eye. Felt like a log or a boulder as it had me tearing up something fierce!

What is a Santa to do?

May God keep that little girl's Mother safe and return her whole and healthy. As the Patron Saint for all service men and women in uniform, may my prayer be heard?

PERSONAL ENCOUNTERS: IT ALL WORKS OUT

Yesterday I had a young man (18 years old) come in with his mother to get a picture taken. He weighed 85 pounds and had palsy. We first tried to have him in his chair next to me but he kept looking to the side away from me. Then we tried him in my chair and his mother lifted him up in her arms and carried him to the Big Chair. He seemed to like that but it was too big for his safety. So we put him back in his chair and positioned him on my other side and he had the biggest smile I had ever seen! It all worked out.

I then dealt with the problems of a child that was 2 years old and blind. He saw my beard through his fingers, then the different textures of the suit from the fur to the velvet. He also checked out the gloves as well. Like any 2 year old he was a little nervous at first but with Mom there with him, it all worked out.

Then it was on to the little boy (5 years old) whose father was in jail. His older cousin (9 years old) was here but her father was living in Mexico and could not come up to see her anymore. We talked about how sometimes Daddy s made mistakes but they always loved their children. With a hug and listening to a few requests, it all worked out.

Later I had a family that was living in a motel room. Their house had burned down and the children were worried that I would not find them Christmas Eve. A few hugs, a couple of stories and it all worked out.

Last I had a little girl who asked for her mother to be home for Christmas. We talked about her Aunt that had escorted her to visit me and so I waived the Aunt over. The little girl and I joke about how her "ant" didn't have 6 legs, and she wasn't all red, and she didn't live in an ant farm. We were all laughing about that and then we talked about the little girl's mother. Mom was in Cedars Sinai Hospital with leukemia. I immediately assured the little girl that her mother was in one of the VERY BEST places to be as an adult! I also told her that not even Santa could contradict the orders of the doctors treating her Mother but that I would do everything I could to help her see her mother on Christmas Day. After the Aunt sent her to look at the pictures, we talked quietly about the Mom and what was happening. For the little girl it all worked out.

I see many children every day while I am sitting in the mall. Most of them just want to give me their requests for toys and get a hug. They are cherished and given the due attention that is expected from Santa when he is busy. Then there are the Children that take a little more time and effort to care for. I spend as much time as needed to make sure they are as happy and secure as I can facilitate.

Sometimes that gets me a fishy stare from my manager for taking too long, but then I explain why and it all works out.

Made in the USA
San Bernardino, CA
15 February 2015